HOW TO COMMUNICATE EFFECTIVELY

The definitive guide on how to communicate effectively, assertively and persuasively. Techniques and strategies to improve communication and achieve your success goals.

Donna V. Carter

Introduction

Communication is the basis of every relationship; in fact, all of us communicate every second of our day both verbally and non-verbally, to express everything that comes into our heads, our emotions but also our needs. Communication can be defined as something purely "human" that we use every day to create, destroy, nourish, change or reconnect our relationships. In psychology, in fact, "being in communication" means that, within communication and through it, each of us forms, nourishes, maintains or changes our own network of relationships.

Network of relationships that we ourselves have contributed to weaving. Simply put, any relationship we want to undertake, or have undertaken, necessarily passes through the path of communication, therefore of the information system that we have transmitted to shape, maintain or modify it. Having made this premise, it becomes logical to think that communication is the foundation of our culture, of our society. Communication in general, in fact, means the transmission of information that passes from an emitter (the starting point) to a receiver (the arrival point). This type of transmission occurs through a sequence of signals subjected to precise coding rules. The main elements that characterize this transmission are:

✓ The source
✓ The transmitter
✓ The channel
✓ The receiver
✓ The recipient
✓ The transducers

Put together, these elements are nothing more than the so-called "communication system". That said, let's think for a moment about what our lives would be like if we couldn't communicate. Now, let's think about being able to do this effectively and how much this would improve our days. Days are centered on messages that we try to continuously convey; sometimes, these messages either don't arrive or are misinterpreted. For a correct interpretation, in fact, a "common code" is always required between the protagonists of the communication, which somehow allows an understanding of the message we are sending. By common communication code we can mean the same language, the typical communication codes of a computer language or any other type of code that must still be understandable between the interactors, precisely because whoever receives the message must be able to decode this message. At this point, communication, and even more so effective communication, is a much more complex phenomenon than it might seem. And here we are at the purpose of this text: to help you improve your lives through effective communication. A type of communication that allows us to get what we want and above all in the correct way. If we manage, as said just above, to convey in a functional way what we want to communicate to our recipient, in a clear and precise way, without ambiguity, don't you also think that you can have much better chances of obtaining that promotion, more collaboration with your partners and so on? We are here to help you! What this practical guide aims to do is to improve your communication system, that coding system in which you will be perfectly able to send the message to your recipient as you wish it to arrive. Furthermore, the message that will reach your recipient must be able to persuade him, that is, bring him to your side without affecting his will. Being able to understand the true art of persuasion will be the other purpose of this text: there will be, in the initial stages of reading, a part dedicated to the distinction between persuasion and manipulation. If your aim is to control others in order to get what you want, without having any qualms, this guide is not for you! Because for us it is essential that you learn to communicate in a persuasive and assertive manner but always with due respect for those in front of you! Because, my dear readers, you cannot spend your life trying to manipulate others by building castles in the air, inventing stories and trying to harm your neighbor: sooner or later this castle will fall and the one who will lose the most will be you, with all the due consequences! What we actually want from you is that you are able to send out a message so clear and specific that the recipient will find it almost elementary to be able to codify it! Thanks to this text, in fact, you will be able to improve your language (both verbal and non-verbal) since it represents the greatest socialization agent.

We will also explain to you what effective communication is and how it arises, what the advantages of using it are, the secrets and techniques for applying it best. There will be a large part dedicated to body language because the fundamental importance of coherence between what we want to communicate and how our body transmits it will be explained to you. You will get what you want and improve your network of relationships. We are sure that, at the end of reading, you will be ready for this! Happy reading and good effective communication!

PART ONE: THE FUNDAMENTALS OF EFFECTIVE COMMUNICATION

In this first part, we will be shown all the basic elements that constitute persuasive and effective communication. We will mainly discuss persuasion, distinguishing it from the "eviler" manipulation, so that you can understand the difference between communicating in a functional way and "controlling" the people we want to interact with. We'll also talk about the benefits of persuasive and effective communication and why you should seriously start practicing improving the ways you deliver your messages immediately!

Chapter 1- Persuasive and effective communication: let's get to know it better

In this first chapter, we will present persuasive and effective communication. Having done this, we will stop to consider the origins of this type of communication and then move on to analyze the constituent elements of this type of communication, namely persuasion and effectiveness. The difference between persuasion and manipulation will also be underlined, because as explained in the introduction, far be it from us to teach you to manipulate others, but to make your communication such that it reaches others without ambiguity and subterfuge.

A little introduction

Before explaining the basic elements of persuasive and effective communication, it is right to give you a short presentation: persuasive and effective communication refers to the ability to activate communicative behaviors with the final aim of transmitting a message capable of inducing a change in the recipient's 'opinion. This change of opinion must occur through a transfer of ideas and a passage of mental contents, precisely clear and efficient. Depending on the objectives set, this type of communication is generally used in marketing or politics. To be able to create this type of communication, which we can also define as "mass" with lots of persuasive power, it took a mix of techniques and knowledge built up over 150 years, all applied in the field of human psychology. Attention, and we want to underline this many times precisely because of its fundamental importance, persuading does not mean "forcing" but simply implies that the recipient of the persuasive and effective communication is free not only to want, to act, but also to think, to believe, to decide based on to what will be communicated to him. Persuading, in fact, as we will see better in the following paragraphs, is just a way to involve the person we are communicating with and perhaps make them change their mind in a completely peaceful way. From here it is easy to deduce that persuasion excludes not only threats and blackmail, but also ambiguous and vexatious moves. Having said this, it can be said that persuasion is more focused on peaceful elements, as anticipated above, on flattery, on the warning against possible future threats and harmful consequences or on the creation of possible future joys, on the unexpressed assumption and on the consequences that are not expressly declared.

In simple terms, therefore, opposite to what one might commonly think, effective and persuasive communication is not a work of forced conviction that does not consider the will and free will of others! Indeed, we can say that persuasion is the cornerstone of efficient communication as it represents something positive, evident and clear and that requires, rather than submission, full collaboration and conscious consent. In addition to these positive elements, persuasion is characterized by the full approval of those with whom we are communicating. In any case, returning to our introduction on effective and persuasive communication, we talk about a key element: the power of communication. This type of power does not reside only in the act of knowing how to speak, but also and above all in the subtle and profound ability to actively listen to others. Active listening is fundamental in any communication system, even more so when it comes to assertive communication; it essentially involves understanding the needs and ideas of those in front of us. By understanding this, we are already halfway there: if we manage to understand our interlocutor and use the right words, we will be able to make him make that decision that he already had in mind, but of which he was not yet convinced. This is a typical marketing technique. This also leads us to show you another key element of effective communication: non-uniqueness, and that is that it must not only be based on us but also on others, through active listening and the ability to understand needs and desires. On the other hand, at least two people communicate; if you communicate alone, you can't even talk about communication! With active listening and the non-unidirectionality of effective communication, the other key element comes into play again, namely the ability to persuade; it is essential precisely because it constitutes the basis of all relationships, both personal and work. In fact, every act of communication requires a certain degree of persuasion to obtain the support and consent of others. And this is why persuading is better than manipulating, because manipulating requires, precisely, univocity, in which only we exist, and we try to force things to be able to obtain what we want. And this is precisely where the problem falls: if people don't understand us or if we fail to understand what they need, the relationship between the two parties struggles to take hold and end in a positive way. Finally, let's examine another fundamental element regarding effective and persuasive communication: its real complexity. We don't want to sugarcoat you, but it's not as simple as it may seem; if you've come this far to read this guide, we're sure there will be some flaw in your communication. Precisely because communicating effectively is not so simple but is the result of a combination of verbal and non-verbal language, in which we try to eliminate any background noise that creates both external (environmental) and internal interference. Easier said than done, right? And that's why, we repeat, we wrote this guide, to ensure that you can put all these complex elements together and create the perfect recipe to be an expert, efficient and successful communicators. At this point, it is essential to communicate in practice through the knowledge and application of specific strategies that will be illustrated in the next chapters of this practical guide! Now, let's continue with the origins of this type of communication.

Origins of persuasion and persuasive and effective communication

Let's now see together what the origins of persuasion and the consequent persuasive and effective communication are. Above, the invitation had already been made to you to abandon any type of manipulation and rather listen to whoever is in front of you and perfectly respect their needs and wishes. To continue the path of correct persuasive communication, therefore, it is necessary to fully understand the art of persuasion. To fully understand this type of art, at this point in the discussion, it becomes equally necessary to know the origin of the term and how this type of communicative art has evolved over time. To go back to the origins, we can offer you some practical examples of persuasive communication from the past, but the most striking example is linked to the persuasive art of religion which used, precisely, mere persuasion to convince people to direct related decisions in their daily lives by taking a position based on morality and religious precepts themselves. Another strong example, always linked to religion, are the religious wars, and in particular the crusades; just think of how much persuasion was used to enlist personnel in the army and to carry out valorous deeds and acts, at the expense of their own safety, to conquer the so-called " Holy Land". Or again we can mention the persuasive art typical of narrators, even more so, going back in time, that typical of the narrators of ancient Greece. These narrators, with precise persuasive narrative mechanisms, managed to enchant those who listened to them with the fantastic strength of their stories, depicting the most heroic deeds. Or the medieval storytellers (the so-called storytellers), in feudal times who always had the ability to arouse emotion in any type of audience. From the most undecided to the most bitter opponents of their master, these storytellers managed to convince even the most resistant audiences in the direction of the master who had employed them the most. From these historical examples it can be deduced that persuasion is an ancient art, and man has always used it to achieve his communicative goals. Going back, the greatest communicators in history were skilled above all at persuading. Always referring to antiquity and taking ancient Greece and ancient Rome as points of reference, we cannot fail to mention two prominent figures.

The first is the philosopher Aristotle, who dedicated one of his most important and famous works to rhetoric. Rhetoric is still used today to understand the mechanisms of persuasive communication. Specifically, Aristotle found a way to organically list all the essential points to keep in mind when starting a speech and to successfully defend the position taken for this speech. Another character absolutely worth mentioning, who continued in the wake of the established rhetoric from Aristotle, is the jurist, writer and philosopher of ancient Rome, Marcus Tullius Cicero. He wrote a work totally in defense of rhetoric, known precisely as the "De Oratore". According to Cicero, a good speech can be prepared at the table or carried out through improvisation, if there is good basic preparation at a cultural level. Again, according to the Roman jurist, the orator par excellence must be very skilled in constructing his speech using three fundamental categories:

1. Invention
2. Disposition
3. Memory.

These three fundamental categories are nothing more than the list of topics, their correct arrangement in the speech, and the use of metaphors to make the speech richer and more articulated. However, if the speaker wishes to improvise, he must take into consideration the use of simple and easy to-understand words, limit the philosophical arguments, be concise and direct and refer to a scheme that must preserve the elocution, the topics of discussion and their declamation. In essence, for Cicero the good orator must be the practical and living example of the values that he tries to promote to those who listen to him. Rules that we can still consider completely valid today! Having closed this brief digression, we can say, however, that persuasive art has not stopped only at heroic deeds and the great communicators of the past but has evolved and been shaped according to our modern needs. The advent of the masses, and the enlargement of the vote, required considerable communication and persuasive skills. And in this regard, tools were sought that could increase effectiveness. One of these tools for persuasive purposes is certainly cinema.

Cinema is in fact a communication tool based on large-scale persuasion. Do you want a striking example here too? Simply mention Disney. Did you think it was invented simply to entertain a younger audience? You are wrong! One of the Disney characters most loved by the public, he served the purpose of propaganda in the United States during the Second World War. The propaganda was aimed at selling emergency government bonds. To date, persuasion, as has already been reiterated previously, is a communication tool widely used by politicians and those who work in marketing, to try to understand the values, needs and choices of recipients to direct them towards what in reality they already want.

And why shouldn't you use it too to get what you want in a clear and completely clean way? In the next paragraph we will delve even further into the topic of persuasion.

What is persuasion?

To provide you with a definition of persuasion that is as close to reality as possible, but also more plausible, we need to go back in time and quote Aristotle again. According to the Greek philosopher, in fact, persuasion is defined as we know it today, that is, the mere art of inducing people to carry out certain actions that they normally would not do if we were not asking them (or inviting them to do so). This definition is what happens with persuasion. Modernizing and adapting it even more to our reality today, we can instead quote Richard Perloff and, specifically, a quote from his book "The Dynamics of Persuasion:

Communication and Attitudes in the 21st Century". In this quote, it is clear that persuasion is nothing more than "a symbolic process in which communicators attempt to convince other people to change their attitudes or behavior when faced with a specific problem, through the transmission of a message in a climate of free choice".

Here, do you see how free choice will remains the cornerstone of persuasive art? Because, contrary to what many people believe, persuasion is neither something mysterious nor wrong, and even less coercive. Many confuse it with less benevolent manipulation. In fact, it is often believed that persuasion is a set of subtle methods with the aim of achieving something that would otherwise have been impossible to obtain without using all these means; but manipulation, believe us, is a special case!

The victims of this "discrimination" or simply of this misunderstanding are the sellers, as they dispense effective and persuasive communication techniques to obtain good results and make more sales. But they are not actually manipulators; we definitely leave this petty art for human relationships, those that we can definitely define as toxic!

However, this does not exclude the not always positive intentions of persuasion. Let's explain better: even if persuasion is considered a neutral tool, it cannot always lead to pleasant or positive results; there are cases in which the results can even be unpleasant. This is to make you understand that everything depends on how persuasion is used and the goals we set ourselves. Now, what we want from you is that you learn to use persuasion effectively. As you will see, to do this you need great listening skills and excellent communication skills. In other words, we are talking about the ability to understand and listen deeply to your interlocutor to understand their needs and requirements and to use this information not to harm or manipulate, but to persuade them to make the right decision. To clarify any doubts, in the next paragraph we will explain in detail what the difference is between manipulation and persuasion.

Persuasion and manipulation: we understand the difference

From what we said above, persuasion and manipulation are often understood as synonyms. Or it is thought, in a very prejudicial way, that both are tools (obviously negative) available to unscrupulous salesmen, tele-salesmen or real estate agents to trample on any type of resistance on the part of customers, making it easier, if not inevitable, to close the contract business and subsequent sale. And this without taking into account the needs, the economic availability of potential customers and what they really want.

This concept of not taking the other into account, let's be careful, leaving aside the active listening part, is the one typically associated with manipulators. The difference with persuasion lies right there: those who persuade take the other person into account and, as we have already reiterated several times, listen to them to understand where to go to persuade, also considering their will. In manipulation no, the other does not exist! Only we exist, with a specific purpose, who try to make others make the most convenient decisions for us: it doesn't matter that the other suffers, or that his will is completely nullified. This is manipulation, and fortunately not all of us are manipulators. Although it must be said that in life, we have all been, more or less, both persuasive and manipulative. Whether it was approving a work project, choosing which restaurant to go to with your partner or which film to see at the cinema, everyone is trying to convince someone to do something. In other words, each of us has used communication to convey our ideas and beliefs, but often done in a completely innocent way. Persuasion is when we try to convince someone of something, considering their needs not univocally but bidirectionally.

The intent behind the convincing action also represents one of the main differences between persuasion and manipulation. The very tools of language used behind these actions can be persuasive or manipulative. In fact, an I-win-you-win relationship is established, that is, my intention involves both a benefit for me and for you and this benefit can be defined as equivalent. There is therefore a positive intention that wants a real improvement in the lives of both protagonists of the relationship. The intent of manipulation, however, is to try to impose something on our interlocutor, considering, as we said above, only our needs and our gain, in an I win-you lose relationship. Now, you may be wondering, why are the two concepts confused so often? Precisely because of a difficulty in distinguishing behavior: two people, in fact, can apparently behave in the same way, but it is their intention that completely changes the meaning of their gesture. You need to be good at understanding intentions. Therefore, to be able to understand whether we have a persuader or a manipulator in front of us, it is necessary to learn the first type of techniques. This is because we find it easier to help others if they are not willing to make a decision that we believe is the right one. But another valid reason is linked to the fact that, being tools that can be used with manipulative intentions, recognizing and neutralizing them can help us defend ourselves from evil people.

Basic elements of effective and persuasive communication

Now that we have well understood the fundamental difference between manipulation and persuasion, let's return to the topic of effective and persuasive communication. It is clear that these are two very distinct realities. Let's see what the basic elements are that characterize persuasive and effective communication. Without going into too much detail, we will briefly show you the various key elements of persuasive and effective communication. In practice you will have to use these elements:

✓ Clarity: it is simply a matter of always expressing oneself in a clear and concise way, avoiding ambiguity. To do this you must therefore use simple and understandable language.

✓ Empathy: as we said previously, our interlocutor matters, with all his needs and desires, and based on the latter it will be necessary to adapt our message and show empathy to create deeper and more profitable connections.

✓ Linked to the above, use active listening. Therefore, pay more attention to what others say and act accordingly and above all appropriately. Active listening improves mutual understanding and makes communication significantly more effective.

✓ The structure of the message must be logical. Therefore, organize your message logically, with a clear beginning, development and conclusion. This makes it easier to follow our reasoning and convey to others what we actually want to communicate.

✓ Emotional involvement: it is simply a matter of using stories, examples and images to emotionally involve our interlocutors. Emotions are powerful in persuading and directing those in front of us.

✓ Credibility: demonstrate, in practice, your competence and reliability to gain the trust of those who listen to us. In this regard, relevant data, testimonials or experiences must be used.

✓ Adaptability: we also need to be flexible and adapt our message based on the context and reactions of our audience. Being adaptable increases our communication effectiveness and is a basic rule (we will explain it better below).

✓ Feedback: Request and accept feedback constructively. This will help us improve our communication over time and make it more effective. This is also a basic rule to learn properly and which we will delve into in the next subparagraph.

4 rules to keep in mind

Let's see what the four basic rules are, to always keep in mind when it comes to having to communicate with others in an effective and persuasive way. The four rules are:

1. Be flexible.
2. Be willing to request and receive feedback.
3. Be assertive.
4. Be positive in communicating.

Let's analyze these four fundamental rules in detail.

Be flexible

Let's start by being flexible. Adaptability is key when trying to communicate effectively. It implies the ability to modify our approach based on the context and dynamics of communication. In fact, people have different communication styles. Being flexible allows us to adapt our message to meet the specific needs of various recipients. But it also allows us to deal with sudden changes. Unforeseen situations, in fact, may require rapid adaptation to our message. Flexibility essentially allows us to manage these variations effectively. Depending on the objectives of our communication, we may find ourselves faced with different situations in which we will be forced to adjust the tone, approach or presentation. In this case, flexibility allows us to achieve our goals in different ways. We also think about possible changes in the context:

20

environmental or situational conditions can indeed vary. Being flexible is also a quality that, in one way or another, makes us capable of adapting our message to unforeseen circumstances. In summary, flexibility in communication allows us to maintain an effective dialogue in a variety of situations, increasing the likelihood of conveying our message clearly and persuasively.

Be able to request and receive feedback

Another rule to always keep in mind is to receive feedback; this is a truly relevant element when it comes to improving our persuasive and effective communication.

Being able to request and receive feedback, however, also requires essential rules. Let's see which ones:

✓ Open reception: the first thing you must do is to always welcome any feedback received with openness and without adopting defensive attitudes. In other words, you should treat every comment as an opportunity to grow and perfect your communication skills. An open attitude towards feedback is essential to becoming a more persuasive and effective communicator over time.

✓ Constructive analysis: Always try to understand the meaning behind the feedback. To do this, never be afraid to ask for clarification if necessary. Once done, reflect on how the suggestions received can be applied to improve our communication approach.

✓ Focus on specific aspects: this involves requesting specific feedback on key elements of our communication, such as the clarity of the message, the structure or the persuasive effectiveness. This will help us shift and concentrate our focus on specific areas for improvement.

✓ Audience observation. We, too, must do our part, observing the reactions of our audience during communication, and then using this information as instant feedback. Facial expressions, body language and questions can provide valuable information to make our communication even more persuasive and effective.

✓ Anonymous feedback: If possible, also encourage anonymous feedback. This can help people be more honest and open in sharing their opinions, thus helping to improve our communication.

✓ Continuous interaction: Consider your communication as an evolving process. To do this, use feedback to make consistent improvements over time rather than treating it as a one-time assessment.

✓ Controlled experiments: Implement changes based on feedback in small steps and see how they affect our communication. This allows us to evaluate the effectiveness of changes without making radical changes.

Be assertive

Being assertive in persuasive and effective communication is another basic rule and serves to express our information and needs clearly and resolutely, while at the same time respecting others. Being assertive in persuasive communication not only increases the likelihood of having our message accepted, but also contributes to building healthier and more respectful relationships.

Assertive communication will be explored in depth in the last paragraph of this chapter. Here we pause to provide you with some guidelines for developing an assertive approach:

- ✓ Clarity and firmness in our message: it is simply a matter of expressing our ideas clearly and directly. In other words, assertiveness requires our message to be unambiguous, highlighting what we believe is important.
- ✓ Clear Position: Always show confidence in your position. Above all, be aware of your rights and opinions, without ever apologizing for having expressed them.
- ✓ Active Listening: in our case, it involves doing two things at the same time. On the one hand we express our ideas, but on the other, we listen carefully to others. Assertiveness does not mean ignoring other people's opinions, but rather establishing a constructive dialogue.
- ✓ Using "I" Statements: Communicate your point of view using statements that begin with "I." For example, instead of saying "You're always wrong," you can say "I get frustrated when..."
- ✓ Flexibility: Being assertive does not mean being rigid. Again, showing flexibility and openness to compromise, if appropriate, allows us to be assertive without compromising our core values.
- ✓ Mutual respect: Always respect the opinions of others even if you don't agree. Assertiveness does not imply disrespect, but rather recognition of different perspectives.
- ✓ Avoid Aggression or Passivity: The rule dictates that you always find a balance between aggression and passivity. Never suppress your opinions, but also avoid overwhelming others with your point of view.

To be positive

Integrating positivity into our communication can greatly improve our ability to persuade and be effective. In fact, integrating positivity into our communication not only makes our message more pleasant, but can also increase our influence and persuasion. This is because positivity always inspires trust and collaboration. How to be one? Here's how to build a positive and constructive dialogue:

- ✓ Positive Tone: Always use an optimistic and encouraging tone. People tend to be more open and receptive when they perceive a positive approach.
- ✓ Positive Language: Opt for words and phrases that convey positive energy. Avoid negative or critical language that could arouse defensive reactions.
- ✓ Focus on Solutions: Instead of focusing on problems, emphasize solutions. Present constructive ideas and proposals that can solve current challenges.
- ✓ Always Underline Strong Points: highlight the strong points of your arguments or proposals. This helps build trust and acceptance of your message.
- ✓ Use positive examples to highlight the benefits of your ideas. This can inspire confidence and demonstrate the validity of your proposals.

- ✓ Express gratitude when you feel it is appropriate. Recognizing the efforts or positive qualities in others helps create a positive climate.
- ✓ Be Optimistic but Realistic: Show optimism but avoid excessive idealism. A positive perspective must be anchored in reality to be credible.
- ✓ Smile and Use Eye Contact: In the case of visual communication or in face-to-face situations, smiling and positive eye contact can significantly improve our expressiveness.
- ✓ Show Appreciation: So, recognize the contributions of others and show appreciation. This helps build positive relationships.
- ✓ Maintain an Open attitude: Also, in this case you need to be open to other people's ideas and accept feedback in a constructive way. This shows maturity and open-mindedness.

How does it work specifically?

Let's start with the definition of communication itself: communicating means putting together, exchanging information, knowledge, needs, attitudes, and emotions, between two or more interlocutors. It is therefore not only, as we have already seen, a one-way passage but an active exchange of questions and answers. This exchange will then serve to make the message clear to all those participating in it. Being open therefore becomes the cornerstone of persuasive and effective communication. In fact, to work best, effective and persuasive communication is open to the point of view of others, to ensure that the person who uses it can increase the chances that their interlocutor will do what they want or see things in the same way as the persuader sees them. Still on the subject of how effective communication works, in addition to language we should also use other tools, such as body language, in a more conscious and controlled way. Using persuasion as a communication technique presupposes perfect knowledge of its principles and its techniques, as well as constant training in the use of both communication and one's own psychic and emotional balance. Communication, effective and persuasive, is essentially conveyed through three main channels:

The verbal channel: Is an essential process that involves the use of words to express thoughts, ideas and emotions. It is a fundamental channel in human interactions, allowing the transmission of information in a clear and understandable way. The effectiveness of verbal communication depends on the choice of words, the tone, the intonation and the context in which it occurs.

The non-verbal channel: this includes gestures, facial expressions, body language, eye contact and other signals not expressed through words. These elements contribute significantly to the transmission of messages and the interpretation of meaning in human interactions. Nonverbal communication can emphasize, complement or even contrast the verbal message, greatly influencing the overall perception of the communication.

The paraverbal channel: Concerns the vocal elements of communication, such as tone of voice, rhythm, volume and intonation. These factors influence the perception and interpretation of the verbal message. For example, a gentle tone of voice can convey calm and friendliness, while a more assertive tone could indicate confidence. The combination of the verbal, non-verbal and paraverbal channels contributes to complete and effective communication.

Before concluding: what is assertive communication?

Assertive communication is a communication style that involves the direct and clear expression of one's opinions, feelings and needs, while respecting others. Assertive communication is of fundamental importance in interpersonal and professional relationships, as it helps to build trust, promote mutual understanding and manage conflicts constructively.

Those who communicate assertively are able to express themselves authentically without violating the rights of others. This communication style involves the ability to defend one's opinions without being aggressive, listen to others with empathy and respond constructively.

Key elements of assertive communication include:

✓ Direct Expression: Communicating your ideas and feelings openly without ambiguity.

✓ Mutual respect: Recognize and respect the rights and opinions of others.

✓ Active listening: Paying attention to the opinions of others in an empathetic and open way.

✓ Emotion Management: Expressing emotions appropriately without repressing or overwhelming others.

✓ Clear communication style: Use clear and direct language, avoiding ambiguity or ambiguity.

Persuasive and assertive communication share the goal of influencing others but differ in their approaches and intent. Persuasive communication, as we have already seen, aims to convince or persuade others to adopt a certain idea, point of view or behavior. In contrast, assertive communication focuses on clarity, directly expressing one's opinions, and defending one's rights without compromising the rights of others. Individuals who communicate assertively seek to assert their opinions in a respectful manner, but do not necessarily seek to persuade or convince others.

In summary, while persuasive communication aims to obtain the agreement or change of opinion of others, assertive communication focuses on the clarity and authentic expression of one's ideas without necessarily trying to influence others. Both styles can coexist, depending on the context and objectives of the communication.

In this chapter we have analyzed all the basic elements that comprise persuasive and effective communication. We have also been able to see that persuasive communication is the ability to activate communicative behaviors with the aim of transmitting a message that can induce a change in the opinion of others. It was also highlighted how persuasion is different from manipulation as it is not based on forced belief, but on free choice and therefore the two concepts should not be confused.

Another point to keep in mind is the difference between communication and persuasive communication. While communication uses only the verbal register, persuasive communication uses both the verbal register, but also the non-verbal and paraverbal ones. The differentiation with assertive communication was also underlined, which is fundamentally based on asserting one's ideas in a clear, direct way but always with respect for others. You were also shown what the basic rules are to follow to create persuasive and effective communication. It is all very theorical, we know, but it is useful to have a complete picture of our main topic. In the next chapter, always in theory, you will be shown all the reasons and advantages associated with persuasive and effective communication.

Chapter 2: The importance and advantages of effective and persuasive communication

In this short chapter we will explain the importance and reasons why you should learn to use a type of communication that is both effective and persuasive. You will see how many areas of life it can help us improve and get what we want. We will also review all the advantages of this type of communication.

We explain why it is important to communicate effectively and persuasively

The transmission of our information through effective and persuasive communication is of fundamental importance today because, first of all, it allows us to convey messages and points of view to any interlocutor. It also offers us the full possibility of transmitting these messages in a manner consistent with our own principles and states of mind. We have already emphasized the equally important importance of body language, which must always be in line with what we want to express. This serves to give strong coherence to our message, but we will talk about this later. Returning to the discussion on the importance of making our communication effective first and foremost, we can say that what makes it so fundamental is linked to the fact that it facilitates mutual understanding, reduces misunderstandings and promotes more positive relationships. In a professional setting, improving communication can increase efficiency and collaboration between team members. In general, clear and accurate communication helps build more constructive, fruitful and beneficial connections in relationships, whether personal or professional.

On the other hand, persuasive communication is equally important because, as we have already explained previously, it allows you to influence the opinions, decisions and behaviors of others in a positive way. When you communicate persuasively, you can achieve desired results more easily by convincing others to adopt certain points of view or take specific actions. This skill is particularly useful in contexts such as business persuasion, leadership and negotiation, helping to achieve common goals more effectively. Persuasive communication can therefore have a really positive impact on your social and working life and, with practice, anyone can develop these skills.

United, these two types of communication will not only make our professional life better but will also allow us to achieve other types of objectives, such as a stable, fulfilling relationship and above all happiness. This is because it is able to make us develop charisma: when, in fact, we become capable of easily convincing people and convincing them to share our vision and our ideas it is as if this affects our personality, as if we were seen from a extraordinary, full of charisma. Charisma, with all its qualities, will be a concept that will be explained better in the last bonus chapter of this guide. Furthermore, we can also say that knowing how to communicate in this way leads us to develop the art of manipulation but, be careful, we are talking about the positive one. In other words, when we manipulate someone in a positive way, we do it first and foremost in a completely open manner and with the sole purpose of doing them good. In fact, to ensure that the manipulation is positive, it is necessary to have a strong sense of self-control and discipline, the result of work on oneself, and everything must always be controlled with caution, especially if one wants to obtain a positive result. A final reason why it is really important to learn to communicate in the best way is linked to our recognizability. We explain ourselves even better: when we communicate to others as if we always understood them perfectly and recognized their desires and needs firsthand, we become immediately recognizable people. In this way you will attract many more people to you, both from the point of view of social relationships and from a work point of view: but we are talking about positive relationships. Therefore, learning to communicate in a persuasive and effective way brings, as we will see further below, many advantages. You have everything to gain!

The advantages of knowing how to communicate effectively and persuasively

Knowing how to communicate adequately offers us enormous advantages, both in the professional and private spheres. Let's distinguish the two areas for a moment.

In the professional field it allows us to:

✓ Increase teamwork skills, improve customer relationships and increase customer loyalty.

✓ Having a positive influence, as it allows us to influence people in a positive way, facilitating understanding and encouraging acceptance of the ideas or proposals presented.

✓ In the workplace, effective and persuasive communication can promote success, improve career advancement opportunities and facilitating leadership.

✓ Contribute to building solid and positive relationships on both a personal and professional level, based on mutual understanding and trust.

✓ Have quick conflict resolution. Effective communication can help resolve conflicts more quickly and efficiently, avoiding misunderstandings and facilitate collaboration. All this can really make work more pleasant and avoid misunderstandings, personal conflicts and wasted time.

✓ Drastically improve the quality and quantity of relationships within the work context.

✓ Have greater negotiating power, as even in the most complicated negotiation situations, persuasion can prove decisive in obtaining advantageous agreements and reaching satisfactory compromises for all parties involved.

✓ Acquire leadership skills, as being able to communicate persuasively is a key trait for a leader and allows you to inspire and motivate others to achieve common goals.

- ✓ Convey professionalism, trust and competence.
- ✓ Have more influence on others: If we are honest, thoughtful and responsible towards others, we are more likely to engage them, arrive at acceptable compromises and get more from them.
- ✓ Recognizes and constructively manages conflicts: each of us has different talents and abilities; therefore, by working together we can achieve goals that we could never achieve alone. But others are also different from us in terms of interests, needs, and values; it is natural that interpersonal conflicts arise. Good communication is therefore an excellent antidote to conflicts and is also the basis for their constructive management.
- ✓ Generate interest, participation and follow-up.
- ✓ Be convincing and achieve excellent results in negotiations.

Communicating in a persuasive and effective way also offers various advantages in interpersonal relationships such as:

- ✓ Have a better understanding of each other. Clear and persuasive communication promotes better understanding between people, reducing the possibility of misunderstandings and conflicts.
- ✓ Building trust: Being able to express ideas convincingly helps build trust in relationships, as people are more likely to trust those who communicate transparently and convincingly.
- ✓ The ability to persuade can help manage and resolve conflicts more effectively, seeking solutions that are acceptable to both parties involved.
- ✓ In personal relationships, persuasion is useful for reaching satisfactory compromises, allowing different perspectives and needs to be reconciled.
- ✓ Develop a greater level of empathy: communicating persuasively and effectively often involves greater awareness of the needs and points of view of others, promoting empathy and mutual understanding.
- ✓ The ability to persuade can be used to inspire and motivate others, helping to generate a positive impact on their choices and actions.
- ✓ It allows us to reach a state of mental peace: Since the way we treat others reflects on our mental and emotional state, a calm and creative way of relating to others will help lower our stress level and make us feel better.
- ✓ Deeper connections with others: Modern life is so full of entertainment and distractions. Instead, learning to listen carefully and express ourselves effectively (two fundamental skills of persuasive communication) allows us to come into deeper contact with ourselves and others.
- ✓ Understand and use body language. That is, learning to understand the intentions, expectations and thoughts of the interlocutors by observing their looks, signs, positions and movements.
- ✓ Building healthy and mentally fulfilling bonds: Persuasive communication can help create stronger and deeper bonds in personal relationships, as it allows you to express feelings, desires and opinions in a convincing way.

also depends on what is called non-verbal communication and listening. Knowing how to communicate therefore also implies knowing how to listen, not in a non-specific way, but through active listening. Furthermore, it means, as we have already said several times, knowing how to use your body language, in order to strengthen and make our message coherent.

Verbal communication, in practice, is only a small part of the communication process. Let's think about the most successful leaders: their charm comes not only from what they say, but also from how they say it. In fact, they use every aspect of communication to establish and build profitable working relationships, or to convey their political ideas, or to promote a collaboration that will benefit different parties. Persuasive communication, as it should be, really works to enter into relationships with people, to be able to understand each other, to facilitate collaboration with the aim of achieving common and shared objectives. And this is what it really means to communicate effectively and persuasively.

What are the objectives of persuasive communication?

Having clarified the concept of the true meaning of effective and persuasive communication, let's see what its main objectives are in detail:

Stimulate the attention of others

The absolute first objective of persuasive and effective communication is certainly to attract the attention of others towards us. To do this, and to ensure that your ideas and message can be conveyed properly, you must also present the facts. Facts that must be interesting to stimulate the attention of others. If the facts are clear, interesting and precise we will have the opportunity to capture the attention of the people we are interacting with. To achieve this primary purpose, you can use shared beliefs or ideas and therefore introduce additional information that your listeners were not aware of. The curiosity that the novelty will arouse, in this case, allows us to achieve our goal.

Convince

Once the attention of our potential interlocutor has been captured, the objective of persuasive communication shifts to trying to induce changes in the beliefs or attitudes of those who have turned their attention towards us. This is not the simplest part, but certainly the most relevant, as the objective of convincing is what makes us understand whether our communication is effective and persuasive or not. Here, we need to use all the tools we have available and which we will explain from the next part of the guide onwards; it is a matter of keeping in mind that often those who listen to you may not perfectly understand what we want to communicate, or their prejudice is so strong that it cannot be easily knocked down. For this reason, it is necessary for us to be able to plan valid and unassaila. everyone can listen and understand our words. And we will explain how to do it in the following chap..

The famous call to action

The final objective of persuasive and effective communication is to ensure that the people whose attention we first attracted and then convinced to come over to our side, move directly into action. The call to action is the precise moment of our speech in which we invite people to actively participate, to always attract and maintain their attention. The call to action, be very careful, must always be clear; therefore, it will be necessary to clearly indicate what we want our interlocutor to do after the communication.

The purpose of the call to action is to create curiosity, solve problems or propose alternatives and solutions. And make sure that we can reach the final goal of our communication.

Things to do in effective and persuasive communication

Now that we know the objectives of our communication, we invite you to pay maximum attention to what you should and should not do to ensure that your message reaches the recipient as it should.

For effective and persuasive communication, it is necessary to focus on the points that we will analyze below:

Clarity and logic

The first thing we must do when communicating effectively is to create clarity and logic in what we are saying. We must therefore be clear and concise to avoid misunderstandings.

It must be said, however, that our ideas and our message must absolutely have some logical structure. It's about organizing our ideas in a sequential and logical way to make it easier to follow our entire speech.

Be well prepared for everything

Here we talk about global preparation, which goes from perfect knowledge of what we want to communicate to the elimination of various obstacles. On the one hand we are talking about in-depth research: in other words, it is about preparing the ground with comprehensive research to demonstrate our competence and mastery of the topic. On the other hand, we are talking about objection management. To break down obstacles we should be perfectly able to anticipate and address possible objections, providing persuasive arguments to overcome them.

PART TWO - ACQUIRING THE TOOLS TO BECOME AN EFFECTIVE AND PERSUASIVE COMMUNICATOR

Now that, in theory, we have understood the basis of effective and persuasive communication, the time has come to explain how it should be used, starting from the objectives of this type of communication and how to achieve it. The mistakes not to be made will also be underlined to ensure that our communication can bring all the advantages we talked about in the previous chapter.

Chapter 3: Effective and persuasive communication - What to do and what not to do

This third chapter starts with an explanation regarding what it really means to communicate effectively and persuasively, and then moves on to what and what not to do to ensure that you become excellent communicators. This type of communication goals will also be shown. Showing you the general objectives serves the purpose of making you understand if they are perfectly in line with your objectives and, therefore, start making your communication better.

What does it really mean to communicate persuasively and effectively?

In this guide we have already explained to you what effective and persuasive communication is and what the basic elements that constitute it are. Now, what does it really mean to be able to communicate in such a functional and efficient way that you can change the minds of others too (always in a peaceful way, of course!)? To answer this question, which until now might seem obvious but in reality, is not at all, knowing how to communicate effectively means being able to incorporate all aspects and methods of communication. It does not simply mean knowing how to speak well, in a correct, clear and precise manner, but on a global level, it means using all the types of communication at our disposal to make our message effective and obtain what we want with our " to communicate". In simple words, it means using the 3 types of languages we indicated previously: but it involves using them in a completely functional way for our direct purposes. Usually, and mistakenly in fact, when we talk about the act of communicating, we immediately think of words, that is, so-called verbal communication. However, those who communicate effectively and persuasively are not only good at using this form of communication. Knowing how to

- ✓ Promoting Collaboration: Persuasion can facilitate collaboration and cooperation in relationships by encouraging active involvement and mutual participation.
- ✓ Better coordinate our activities with those of the people who are most important to us. Living and working with others are intensely communicative activities. The more we can understand the feelings and desires of others, the more clearly others will be able to understand ours. It will then be easier to navigate together in the same direction.
- ✓ Inspire more respect in others. Much of communication is based on imitation, if we adopt a more attentive and respectful attitude towards others, we incite them, precisely, to behave in the same way towards us.
- ✓ Carrying out interpersonal relationships in the best possible way, or positively influencing the opinions of others, their attitudes and their actions are just some of the countless benefits that can be obtained thanks to good, effective and persuasive communication skills.

In this chapter we have shown how important it is to have excellent communication skills and what benefits we could gain once we learn to use persuasive communication. Persuasive communication is important because it allows us to convey messages and points of view to any interlocutor, in a manner consistent with their principles and moods. Knowing how to communicate effectively will help you in many aspects of your working life, but also in your private life, such as in the education of your children, or in having good relationships with the various members of your family. Therefore, learning to communicate effectively and persuasively offers us a series of incalculable advantages in both our personal and professional lives.

Our first theoretical part of the guide concludes with the importance and advantages of communicating effectively and persuasively. From the next part onwards, everything will become more practical, and you will begin to acquire the tools to build the type of communication that will dramatically improve your life.

communicate also depends on what is called non-verbal communication and listening. Knowing how to communicate therefore also implies knowing how to listen, not in a non-specific way, but through active listening. Furthermore, it means, as we have already said several times, knowing how to use your body language, in order to strengthen and make our message coherent.

Verbal communication, in practice, is only a small part of the communication process. Let's think about the most successful leaders: their charm comes not only from what they say, but also from how they say it. In fact, they use every aspect of communication to establish and build profitable working relationships, or to convey their political ideas, or to promote a collaboration that will benefit different parties. Persuasive communication, as it should be, really works to enter into relationships with people, to be able to understand each other, to facilitate collaboration with the aim of achieving common and shared objectives. And this is what it really means to communicate effectively and persuasively.

What are the objectives of persuasive communication?

Having clarified the concept of the true meaning of effective and persuasive communication, let's see what its main objectives are in detail:

Stimulate the attention of others

The absolute first objective of persuasive and effective communication is certainly to attract the attention of others towards us. To do this, and to ensure that your ideas and message can be conveyed properly, you must also present the facts. Facts that must be interesting to stimulate the attention of others. If the facts are clear, interesting and precise we will have the opportunity to capture the attention of the people we are interacting with. To achieve this primary purpose, you can use shared beliefs or ideas and therefore introduce additional information that your listeners were not aware of. The curiosity that the novelty will arouse, in this case, allows us to achieve our goal.

Convince

Once the attention of our potential interlocutor has been captured, the objective of persuasive communication shifts to trying to induce changes in the beliefs or attitudes of those who have turned their attention towards us. This is not the simplest part, but certainly the most relevant, as the objective of convincing is what makes us understand whether our communication is effective and persuasive or not. Here, we need to use all the tools we have available and which we will explain from the next part of the guide onwards; it is a matter of keeping in mind that often those who listen to you may not perfectly understand what we want to communicate, or their prejudice is so strong that it cannot be easily knocked down. For this reason, it is necessary for us to be able to plan valid and unassailable points so that everyone can listen and understand our words. And we will explain how to do it in the following chapters.

The famous call to action

The final objective of persuasive and effective communication is to ensure that the people whose attention we first attracted and then convinced to come over to our side, move directly into action. The call to action is the precise moment of our speech in which we invite people to actively participate, to always attract and maintain their attention. The call to action, be very careful, must always be clear; therefore, it will be necessary to clearly indicate what we want our interlocutor to do after the communication.

The purpose of the call to action is to create curiosity, solve problems or propose alternatives and solutions. And make sure that we can reach the final goal of our communication.

Things to do in effective and persuasive communication

Now that we know the objectives of our communication, we invite you to pay maximum attention to what you should and should not do to ensure that your message reaches the recipient as it should.

For effective and persuasive communication, it is necessary to focus on the points that we will analyze below:

Clarity and logic

The first thing we must do when communicating effectively is to create clarity and logic in what we are saying. We must therefore be clear and concise to avoid misunderstandings.

It must be said, however, that our ideas and our message must absolutely have some logical structure. It's about organizing our ideas in a sequential and logical way to make it easier to follow our entire speech.

Be well prepared for everything

Here we talk about global preparation, which goes from perfect knowledge of what we want to communicate to the elimination of various obstacles. On the one hand we are talking about in-depth research: in other words, it is about preparing the ground with comprehensive research to demonstrate our competence and mastery of the topic. On the other hand, we are talking about objection management. To break down obstacles we should be perfectly able to anticipate and address possible objections, providing persuasive arguments to overcome them.

Be flexible

It's about simple adaptability and always being ready to customize and change our approach based on the audience to maximize the impact of the message and ideas we want to convey. Never remain rigid in your positions: understanding what type of audience we are trying to persuade and also changing based on their perspective makes us much better communicators! Another very useful tool that we should always adopt is the monitoring of non-verbal signals. In other words, it involves carefully observing the interlocutor's non-verbal signals to adapt our approach based on their reactions.

Audience knowledge

Speaking of flexibility and adaptability, to ensure that our message is within reach of our audience, we must first understand it in every aspect. Knowing the audience, therefore, is an essential step if we want to achieve excellent communication objectives. With the active listening that we recommended above, it will be possible to understand our audience, their needs, values and concerns. Only then can we adapt our message to make it stand out even more with what is important to them.

Respect for those in front of us

Even when we create a sort of emotional involvement perhaps using stories and examples to emotionally involve the audience, we must be not only clear and credible, but also respectful. It is simply a matter of always using respectful language, but above all avoiding offensive tones to maintain a positive climate. It is also about having respect for other people's time: we must therefore also be respectful of other people's time, keeping our communication focused on the key points without rambling or being confused.

Always accept other people's opinions

It's not just about having respect but also about accepting both praise and constructive criticism. Feedback must never be missing in our process of improving communication. So, accept and integrate feedback to continually improve your communication skills, but also to see where you are in your communication process. Here self-awareness also comes into play; at this point it will be possible to reflect on our communication, identify points for improvement and constantly work on ourselves to refine our persuasive skills, always taking into account the tools and techniques that we will show you later in this guide.

What to avoid in effective and persuasive communication

Now that we know everything there is to do for persuasive and effective communication, let's see what mistakes you should avoid making. Take these errors into account as they could create communication barriers and therefore mislead the message or prevent that emotional bond from forming, that connection that is so crucial to the success of our communication system. This is not something extremely serious, but errors that often make the people we communicate with uncomfortable, even leading to the abrupt interruption of our dialogue. And that's all we want to avoid. So, let's see together what the things are you absolutely must not do if you want to be an efficient and persuasive communicator.

Don't give our full attention to whoever is in front of us

We have already mentioned it several times, the so-called active listening: it is not just us that exists, but communication follows the two-way rule therefore, when we talk to someone, we must make them understand and make them feel that what he or she wants to communicate to us is equally important compared to what we want to tell him. To ensure that you can be good communicators, never forget fairness in communication; if we make it clear to the other person that we are not really listening to them, how can we create that deep bond, that connection that we need to correctly convey our message? It's about taking a simple action: when you are interacting with someone, drop everything you are doing and give them your full attention. It is not just a question of pure and precise respect, but if we want to capture and convince the other person we must make sure that what we want is exactly what she or he wants. This is how persuasion works, the positive one: have you already forgotten? This is why not paying attention, not practicing active listening is one of the most serious mistakes that can be made in proper communication. If we are deficient in this specific activity, we should simply work harder at it.

Disregard other people's concerns

When we interact with another person, we not only have to give them our full attention, but we also have to try to understand how this person is feeling at that precise moment. It's about understanding what they are trying to communicate to us and how they feel about what they are telling us, therefore their concerns and needs. This is also, as we have seen, the objective of active listening just mentioned above. However, we must not only pay initial attention, but we must always let our interlocutor finish speaking without trying to minimize their emotions and concerns. Trying not to interrupt whoever is speaking to us is also an absolutely effective way to demonstrate that we are actively listening, as well as a sign of good manners; not interrupting also shows that we are really interested in what our interlocutor is communicating, creating the connection we need to get what we want from our communication. And always remember:

✓ Avoid changing the subject or minimizing the story of your interlocutors.

✓ If you really can't understand your interlocutors' concerns, you can always ask for clarification.

✓ In any case, respect above all else: always avoid being rude and making people feel uncomfortable. They should feel free to express concerns and emotions.

Judging is not our job

Still on the subject of respect, another very serious mistake we can make is setting ourselves up as judges of the moment. If our goal is precisely to communicate persuasively, judging and criticizing our interlocutors takes us miles and miles away from it. Let us always remember that each of us has different levels of knowledge and different levels of understanding. When understanding fails, and we start judging those who speak or listen to us, perhaps based only on prejudices, we end up lacking respect and offending others who will prefer to abandon the conversation rather than stay in an uncomfortable climate.

Unsolicited advice: red flag

Ah, unsolicited advice – we all love it, right? Irony aside, think about it: no one wants, in addition to being judged, to be told what to do or how to manage their life. We are here to communicate, without cheating, prejudice and arrogance. Therefore, never give unsolicited advice, even if the person in front of you is looking for advice on life. Giving unsolicited life advice to someone who is just looking for comfort or a way to vent may cause them to find our attitude offensive and disrespectful and turn away or reject our message.

It's okay to be prepared, but never use overly technical phrases and terms

We told you that it is right to be perfectly prepared and have a good, if not excellent, command of our ideas and arguments. Warning: this does not mean overdoing it! Using technicalities when talking to someone is the shortest way to make our message incomprehensible and lose their interest. As well as making our conversation boring and confusing.

In this regard, to avoid disaster, we will always try to keep the first point of things to do, holding our speech in a clear and concise way and using simple words that are easy for our interlocutors to understand.

This way you will get what you are looking for without requiring huge efforts.

In this chapter we have explained the things to always keep in mind when talking about persuasive communication and what the objectives are to achieve: stimulating, convincing and inviting action. We have understood the correct actions to take and those to avoid in order to avoid communication errors.

It's about paying due attention to our interlocutor, taking other people's concerns into account, creating connections, but also not judging others, not giving unsolicited advice and above all not speaking in an inappropriate and disrespectful way.

Having closed this discussion, in the fourth chapter we will begin to reveal all the techniques and secrets of persuasive and effective communication: let's keep on!

Chapter 4: Secrets and rules of persuasive and effective communication

In this chapter you will begin to acquire all the valid tools you will need on your journey to learning perfect communication! After having talked about what persuasive communication is and how it was born, and once having established what things to do and mistakes to avoid, it is now necessary to know all the rules and secrets to attract and keep the attention of our interlocutor. As we have seen, the first thing to do is to arouse curiosity and convince our potential interlocutor to carry out the final act or what we wish to obtain from our communication. We will begin this chapter by indicating what persuasion strategies are and then move on to reveal the secrets of effective communication.

A brief introduction to persuasion strategies

Before revealing the secrets and, consequently, the rules for being able to communicate effectively and persuasively, let's talk in general about persuasion techniques and strategies. Using persuasion techniques and strategies means first of all learning to communicate a certain concept, idea or proposal in the best possible way.

If you think about it carefully, only by presenting your product or service to the best of its potential will it allow you to get your message to people. By understanding the potential, the strong points and therefore the possible benefit that can be drawn from it, it will be easier for those in front of us to visualize the product in their hands and how it would improve their life, once purchased.

This is how an effective persuasion technique works. It's nothing that complicated: most persuasive communication techniques, in fact, are quite simple both to understand and to apply in practice. The main difficulty, however, lies in the ability of each of us to master these techniques, with the necessary confidence and faith in success. Being able to persuade those who are listening to us therefore requires a lot of study and above all constant practice. It must never be something far-fetched, but everything must start from the creation of a well-defined strategy and knowing how to master all the objections that may be raised by our interlocutor, in order to also be able to modify our strategy along the way.

It is the famous preparation we talked about in the previous chapter: when we are well decided that we have to "sell" our idea, our project, our service or anything else, we need to study a lot, plan and implement a sales strategy. Forecast that includes possible obstacles, contingencies or objections. Nothing, therefore, must be left to chance: a lot of study, a lot of work, good will and perseverance are needed! We will help you on how to do it, starting by revealing what the secrets of effective and persuasive communication are!

What are the secrets of persuasive and effective communication?

As we have just stated above, effective communication is not an improvised strategy: even when we study and prepare ourselves perfectly for any eventuality, what we have prepared is not valid once and for all, but requires prerogatives, such as flexibility and adaptation. We have already said, the strategy must be flexible, adaptable and moldable based on the audience we have in front of us because every story is subjective, every experience influence communication and therefore also the relationship with others. And this is the second secret we will reveal to you. The first, if it is not yet completely clear, was revealed just above: persuasion, complete with effective communication, only works with excellent preparation. Preparation which, and here the second secret comes into play, must be followed by excellent flexibility which serves to make us review and shape our strategy, based on our interlocutor, his needs and desires but also his possibilities. And here we come to the third secret: ears and eyes open! This simply means applying the famous "active listening" already mentioned previously. Without going into too much detail, it means paying attention to what our potential listener says, understanding their needs and emotions and adapting our strategy based on this collection of information! As you become more and more skilled, you will have developed the strategy to apply based on certain circumstances. Unfortunately, those who do not possess these qualities indicated above (consistency and preparation, adaptability and flexibility, active listening) find it much more difficult to propose their ideas and ensure that they are willingly accepted by others. In such a situation, acquiring good persuasion skills is not easy, but it is not impossible either. Here we would benefit from a process of self-awareness capable of making us understand in which skills we are most lacking and which we are strongest. Once you have learned this, it becomes necessary to know the right techniques and understand the principles that govern this type of communication. We told you: it's also about planning, but proper planning requires a series of rules and strategies. Rules and strategies that we will reveal to you in the next paragraph.

Rules and strategies for effective communication

The only way to ensure that our interlocutor can change his way of seeing and thinking, and making it more like ours, is to master effective and persuasive communication; there's no doubt about this! To create our special communication technique, however, it is necessary to follow very specific rules. After various research, studies and investigations carried out on the best communicators of the moment, we managed to organically collect these rules which, to be precise, are five. These five rules are nothing more than connected to the secrets of persuasive and effective communication indicated above. In any case we have:

1. Empathy.
2. Compassion.
3. Active listening.

4. Attention and concentration.

5. Style and words of communication.

These five rules will have to be imprinted perfectly in your mind. Obviously now we will explain them to you in detail, indicating their main characteristics.

Empathy

The first fundamental rule concerns empathy, or the ability to understand the pain and emotions of others. If you are not empathetic you cannot be good communicators. Sorry! In the field of persuasive communication, empathy is considered, in practice, the opposite of manipulation, because here we take into account the feelings and needs of others. However, it is not just the ability to understand people's moods, but also knowing how to interact with others based on one's own emotions. It is a game of emotions, in which the true skill lies in tuning into other people's emotions and the context in which we are inserting ourselves into the interaction. The first rule, therefore, is to put yourself in the other person's shoes and be able to tune our emotions to theirs! It is the bond and the emotional connection that we have already talked about, since if we are in tune, we have more possibilities to create visualization in the other, giving him only the benefits deriving from what we are transmitting. Now, projecting ourselves into the sphere of reality and seeing it from our point of view, nowadays the so-called empathetic people are the ones who most easily attract our sympathy. Think about it: we usually prefer to deal with people who lift our spirits when we are sad thanks to their good mood, their positivity but above all their full understanding, because with them we can communicate openly, also letting ourselves go into intimate confidences and personal, without fear of judgment and without fear. Because those people understand us, and we will possibly be more inclined to listen to their advice. Having said that, it is now established that being empathetic is essential to being able to persuade someone. At this point, applied to persuasive and effective communication, empathy will first of all help you improve your listening, understanding and empathy skills, which are fundamental for attracting not only the attention of others but also their "sympathies". The people in front of us, when they realize that we care, will feel truly listened to and understood and will be more inclined towards us, as well as listening to us with greater attention and interest. It's a relationship of giving to receive, it's useless! Simply put, if we want to persuade someone, the first essential aspect to consider is the human need for consideration. People want to be considered and understood first and only then will they accept being directed to do what we want. Unless a person is totally at the mercy of others and therefore easily manipulated, people want an exchange relationship! Whoever manages to satisfy this need for consideration will enter the circle of trusted people and will be a point of reference more easily listened to. This is all you need to focus on. However, we want to clarify one thing: we talked about putting yourself in the other person's shoes, but being empathetic when it comes to communicating effectively does not necessarily mean actually putting yourself in the other person's shoes, and above all we must not expect the other to put themselves in our shoes. Let's explain better: the rule of empathy means putting yourself in the other person's shoes, but only to avoid the serious mistake of giving unwanted judgments and advice that can make our interlocutor distance themselves (remember that?). It's about making an effort towards others to establish an open and constructive dialogue, without ever exceeding the limits. The skill of being empathetic in effective and persuasive communication lies precisely in this balance! Start really working on it and the rule is: neither too much nor too little (of empathy obviously).

Compassion

In a current society like ours, where individualism is taken to the extreme, compassion is very often considered the typical characteristic of people with a weak, compliant and condescending character. Obviously, this is just a prejudice; contrary to this erroneous perception, compassionate people are extremely strong people, since they act for the good of others, as well as helping those who have suffered wrong. The negative characteristic is linked precisely to the fact that these are a rather rare type of person! Without digressing too much and returning to the field of communication, we often see subjects who do not show a minimum of compassion, showing an impoverished and destructive way of communicating, probably due to various negative experiences and disappointments. In this case the rule to follow, always and in any case, is to show a type of communication that is empathetic but also compassionate. Compassion, in these cases, is a powerful tool to defuse people who live in a constant state of anxiety and who are excessively distrustful of each other. It is another way, like empathy, of attracting others towards us and creating the famous emotional (and communicative) bond. Understanding, always without expressing any judgment, the fragility of others serves to break down the wall that is created to defend oneself from adversity.

In this regard, the rule of compassion that we should follow must never represent a force but must be taken into strong consideration if we want to achieve a better final goal (i.e. communicate effectively). If we lack it, we should learn genuine and sincere compassion, which will then automatically become a useful tool for considering the emotions of others as precious and highly valuable elements. It must be said, however, that all of this serves us above all for our personal gain: understanding how to protect these emotions will only help us obtain advantages from a communication point of view.

Active listening

We will never tire of repeating it to you; if you don't listen to others you can't communicate! We revealed it to you as a thing to do and as a secret for the success of your communication, now it has become an imperative, the rule to follow. Before speaking, listen, but do so in an active and sincerely interested way. Most people prefer to talk rather than listen, and unfortunately this happens much more often than you might think! Not to mention those who enjoy just hearing their own voice, speaking in endless monologues only about themselves, without ever letting others speak, so that all the attention is focused on them. In addition to being impolite, this attitude denotes a lot of insecurity, typical of those who do not know how to communicate. Let's repeat it again: if you don't know how to listen, you won't know how to communicate! Now that you've probably heard about it, let's dispel another myth: the one about people who prefer to listen to others rather than talk. This rarity is usually considered to have low intellectual content and little argumentative ability. Well, this is a very widespread prejudice that must absolutely be eliminated. Contrary to what is commonly believed, these people in reality often expertly apply active listening. Active listening helps them have control of the entire conversation. Have you ever seen it from this perspective? Thanks to this control, it is possible to find people who are more likely to open up to us. In this way it will be possible for us to learn a lot of crucial information about our interlocutor. Information that will subsequently be used to establish an effective and persuasive communication strategy. However, active listening does not only mean listening carefully and actively to the other, but also acting actively on our part. In other words, active listening does not imply the total silence of the listener, but intervention at the most appropriate moment in the conversation to make it profitable, that is, introducing elements that make our conversation engaging and effective. In practice it involves actively making contributions within the conversation, and this is where we come into play after some listening work, which can help the speaker to open up more or push him to talk about what interests us most. It is a very valuable collection of information that allows us to take another's perspective, understanding and addressing the motivations behind words and their behaviors. In this way, a climate of collaboration and discussion is created which leads the interlocutors to look in the same direction, which is what we need to ensure that our message is effective and persuasive. Whether in a relational or professional context, this type of skill allows us to establish effective connections and achieve our communication goals, also helping us to grow personally.

How to correctly practice active listening?

Having established the full usefulness of active listening and understood the fact that it will always be useful to us, helping us to understand the thoughts and emotions of our interlocutor, we can affirm that this ability allows us to always maintain a high level of attention and connection with those we listen to. How to apply this rule correctly? This rule or skill can be developed and improved through various measures that will help us become more attentive listeners and improve our communication. Let's see, specifically, what are the rules to follow within the "rule" itself:

1. The absolute first step to take is to focus your attention on the other. You have to listen to it really and with interest. No distractions, no strategies for now, it's just a matter of listening and gathering as much as possible useful information. Another mistake you shouldn't make is getting distracted from what you want to say next. For a moment only the other must exist; exclude yourself from the conversation completely!

2. Don't interrupt, ever! Because in addition to, as we have already said previously, being uneducated, it makes us lose focus on the objective. Unless it's been twenty minutes straight and you're making a spider out of a hole. So, there you have to be skilled in getting the person to say what interests you; in this case, with great courtesy, it is possible to introduce the famous elements of information which consist of useful questions to better understand our interlocutor and then direct the conversation towards something that really interests us.

3. Show interest. Here our body language also comes into play: we must express interest in every part of our body so we should carefully look him in the eyes (without exaggerating of course), nod but also be a sort of mirror that reflects his emotions. Interest, in other words, means smiling, rejoicing or being sad, in short, adapting to the emotions of others. Expressing the same emotion, making those in front of us perfectly at ease, will allow us to make others understand that the time has come to create the communicative connection that will then be used to introduce our message.

4. Give an opinion. Opinion, not judgement! Really pay close attention to this small but very important differentiation: on the one hand it is important that our interlocutor sees us alive and active, but that doesn't mean that we have to spit out sentences. We report what he said and refer to his reasoning, without being offensive or disrespectful. An opinion expressed in the best way, in reference to what he or she is saying, will make him or her feel understood and listened to even when we are admitting that we do not agree with him or her. Let's take a practical example to understand each other better: there is a lot of difference in saying "you made a mistake, I would never have done it this way!" or "I absolutely don't agree, what kind of reasoning is that? It would be better to say phrases like "I don't blame you for what you did or what you say, but I don't agree with it!" Do you understand how the second statement sounds a little better? Listen, give opinions but measure words and ways!

5. The importance of "yes". If you are a person who is used to always saying no, or someone who is famous or "very nice" is the opposite, you will never be a good communicator. Positivity and the benevolent power of yes work miracles, believe it! When our interlocutor explains his point of view, it is good to react with a "yes" even if we do not agree with what he has just said. This is not hypocrisy, but simply a correct reaction that will allow us to later resume the conversation with a "yes but...", never with a "no but...". And this makes the difference because our interlocutor will feel as if we are part of the same team and that he does not have to fear a possible contrary opinion, if what he says is not perfectly in line with our communication objectives. The famous persuasive system is therefore also made of yes.

6. Build a possible solution based on the ideas of others. Another rule to follow is to also be flexible within an active listening action. Active listening, in fact, allows us to find different solutions or get a better idea, based on what we are listening to. Has a light bulb ever gone on in your head when you perhaps heard someone else's idea? It is a work of flexibility that leads us to improve an idea we had at the start and adapt it to what the other is communicating to us. You have no idea how many solutions are found

thanks to active listening! Practice more and more to refine this skill and you will see that your communication strategy will improve more and more!

Global Focusing

Once we have finished studying our interlocutors correctly and in depth and established an emotional bond (complete with unconditional trust), we know that listening worked but that the time has come to take action! We are simply talking about the fact that, now that we have captured the attention of our interlocutors and are managing to keep it active, we need to really make ourselves heard. Attracting attention and then keeping it constant on us, however, is not at all simple. Attention is that ability that allows us to select all the elements and information that, when inserted in a certain context, are considered more important than others. Now the rule to follow is that of concentration, to ensure that attention becomes useful to us. The rule of concentration essentially refers to sustained attention that lasts even for a long period of time. To increase and intervene positively on concentration it is necessary to raise the level of motivation, otherwise the main element of attention towards what we now have to say and therefore to communicate is lost. It is essential to understand that the people with whom we interact have different levels in insight. Starting from this assumption, we should be perfectly aware that some may respond slowly to stimuli, requiring continuous and increasing stimuli. Others may suffer from attention deficits, making it difficult to maintain their concentration for long periods. Therefore, considering these differences must be a rule to take into account when communicating and deciding which information is relevant in a certain context. In any case, it becomes truly decisive to make full use of all the linguistic resources available to keep the audience constantly involved. The advice is therefore to focus above all on the first few minutes of the speech, since they can significantly influence the overall success of the message. Make sure the beginning of your speech is clear and understandable. As you continue, carefully monitor your audience's attention and react promptly to signs of waning interest. If you sense that your attention is waning, change your strategy immediately. There are several techniques for capturing or restoring attention during speeches. For example, you can adopt the storytelling technique or share intriguing anecdotes to stimulate listeners' curiosity. The best strategy, in this case, but also the simplest and quickest, is to ask trick questions to your interlocutors to understand if they are really focused on you. Alternatively, in case you notice that your audience's attention is dispersing, you can win them back by asking questions that stimulate their interest. A quick and effective way is to ask engaging questions of those present.

Another strategy to capture attention is to share personal experiences relevant to the environment and topic being discussed. The effectiveness of such stories will be greatest if reflect situations with which the audience can identify.

If you want to consolidate your speech or revive attention, you can illustrate concepts with concrete examples related to the topic covered. The use of images as a support will not only facilitate listening but will also influence the subconscious of the audience. All to understand if now the concentration of other people's attention is fully focused on you and on your goal of communicating effectively and persuasively.

Style and words of communication

The last rule, more than representing a rule, is a truly effective communication strategy. The ability to lead a conversation or give a speech with an effective communication style brings several advantages, since there are no rigid communication rules and offers the communicator greater flexibility. In addition, using a persuasive communication style not only puts the interlocutor at ease, but also encourages him to support the communicator's point of view. Despite the flexibility of this communication approach, it is essential to pay attention to the words used. An effective speech should not be improvised, but must result from study, rehearsal and practice. Depending on the type of speech, it is necessary to replace less incisive words with more impactful alternatives. At the same time, it is advisable to eliminate terms or expressions that could evoke negative situations, replacing them with words that evoke reassuring images in the minds of listeners. Style will be crucial to the success of our conversation.

Our chapter also concludes with the five essential rules of persuasive and effective communication, combined with the secrets to achieve it. In fact, we have listed and explained to you what the secrets of persuasive communication, empathy, compassion, active listening, attention and concentration, communication style and words are. These rules must be followed to the letter if we really want to develop and refine our communication skills. The final advice is not to leave out, skip or ignore any of these rules because everything is connected, and everything is useful for our purpose. Now that we are perfectly aware of what awaits us to plan our best persuasive and effective communication strategy, we will move on to the third part of the guide which will teach you, step by step, all the techniques to achieve your communication objectives.

PART THREE - APPLYING EFFECTIVE AND PERSUASIVE COMMUNICATION TECHNIQUES

Up to now we have analyzed the characteristics, objectives and revealed some secrets of effective and persuasive communication. Now it's time to take all this information and tools, put them together and explain how to apply the best techniques to communicate in such a way that we can get what we want from our listening audience. After having explained the best techniques for communicating to the best of your potential, we will discuss tone of voice and fluidity. You will understand how the importance of applying both aspects can make your conversation decidedly better!

Chapter 5: The best persuasive and effective communication techniques

This fifth chapter will only include a rather long paragraph, where all the best persuasion techniques will be examined and then shown in detail. We have already been able to understand in the course of this guide that, when it comes to persuasion, for many, it is mistakenly just a matter of applying some strategies and tricks to quickly and easily change the thoughts of others, leading them to carry out the actions we desire. As we will explain better below, it is all a little more complicated and very different from this common thought.

Persuasive and effective communication techniques in detail

In the introduction of this chapter, we had already opened the discussion on the fact that persuasion techniques, implemented with the mere aim of making others change, do not work. At least, they don't work alone and are definitely not effective. Of course, persuasion strategies certainly have a fundamental role, but they are of little use if those who apply them do not have the ability to exploit them or do not fully understand what they are for. And especially if they have not been applied in a context of persuasive and effective communication. Having said this, let's now move on to indicate the most used techniques to create perfect, persuasive and effective communication.

The decoy effect

The first technique or strategy we want to analyze is the so-called decoy effect, also known as the "asymmetric dominance effect". In simple words, it is the tendency according to which human beings must find, but above all fish for, opportunities even when they do not present themselves in front of us. And this is perfectly applicable in the field of sales too. In this regard, the decoy effect is the result of a process of direct influence on the decisions and habits of consumers with the introduction of a new alternative, which is not only able to lighten, at least in appearance, the comparison between the two starting products, but also manages to direct our audience to what we would really like to sell! In the world of marketing, if we wanted to give some examples, the bait effect could be represented by the introduction of a very expensive product like another which, in comparison, seems much less expensive, but is actually what we want to promote and sell. In this case the introduction of this more expensive product represents a sort of "distraction" instance with the aim of being a precise stimulus to influence the decision, i.e. the consumption habits of customers. The desired result is not always obtained: in this case the situation will be further directed towards our product with another bait, i.e. the addition of a third unit, which seems to highlight the presumed strengths of one of the two options. This is a type of addressing in reverse: the main objective, in fact, of those who use the bait effect as a persuasion technique in marketing campaigns, is not to direct the individual consumer towards their products, but rather than keep it away from competing ones. By distancing consumers and discouraging them from purchasing the products of competing companies, we will indirectly have the effect of directing their attention towards our product. Therefore, without direct promotion, thanks to the bait effect the result will be what we hope for. Even when we want to convince someone, it is possible to do so by using a comparison that makes our idea much more attractive than those presented by others.

The principle of reciprocity

We have already been able to see during the reading of this book that correct communication is based on an exchange relationship, where we listen to our interlocutor, take into account his feelings and needs and end up making him believe that what is good for us it is equally beneficial for them. It is, essentially, a relationship based on reciprocity, from which the principle as a persuasive and effective communication technique also takes inspiration. Professor of social psychology Robert Cialdini spoke specifically about this principle, referring to that innate mechanism that we human beings possess to reciprocate favors and express reciprocity. A practical example could be a birthday or Christmas gift. If someone gives us a gift, we will also take one in return for the nice gesture, because we feel it is the right thing to do. The principle of reciprocity is also linked to our education. Since we were children, our parents taught us the importance and education of reciprocating a nice gesture, a thought, a gift. These are also lessons in gratitude: we have in fact been taught that, if someone gives us something, as well as trying to reciprocate, we must always thank and be grateful for what we have received. Or we have been taught that if someone does us a favor, we must always return it. Reciprocity is an attitude that we have acquired since childhood, and that is an integral part of our daily lives. Now, it is right that you know that the principle of reciprocity represents one of the best tools to use in persuasive and effective communication. The principle of reciprocity, however, must never be something truly explicit or overbearing, in the sense that we must demand immediate restitution of favor, but it must always be well hidden and used correctly, because people will respond to our stimuli unconsciously. In many cases, reciprocity will occur without the person realizing it and will do so automatically. The strategy based on reciprocity, to give a practical example, is used by some door-to-door sellers, in three simple steps:

✓ First of all, making an excessive request to which, generally, the immediate consequence is a refusal (it is in the face, in fact).

✓ Once the refusal is received, the seller will take care of withdrawing the initial request.

✓ When withdrawn, make a smaller request, which is usually accepted to put the person with innate capacity for reciprocity, to compensate for the initial refusal.

You can also apply these simple moves very well in everyday life: the important thing is to never force things, but to let everything happen randomly and without demanding the impossible from our interlocutor.

The principle of scarcity

Here is another very useful principle in order to be able to communicate effectively and persuasively, namely the principle of scarcity. This persuasion technique is based on the theory that the rarer and more inaccessible something becomes; the more people want it at all costs. And this applies to both material and immaterial things, such as success or experience. This principle, in fact, is widely applied in the field of sales, especially of luxury goods or to grab a niche willing to spend any amount just to obtain the desired product or good.

From a persuasive perspective, therefore, the more we reduce the availability of a product, or the more we make our idea unique, rare and unrepeatable, the more those who listen to you will be inclined to want what we are offering them. A practical example of scarcity can be products with limited availability. If we point out that our products or ideas are in short supply or out of stock, those we want to persuade will be more likely to purchase them to avoid missing the opportunity.

Chameleon effect

The chameleon effect was introduced for the first time by John Bargh, a psychologist at Yale University, stating that we often tend to imitate the postures, mannerisms and facial expressions of those around us, without realizing it, as if, precisely we mold ourselves to those around us. Exactly like the chameleon does: it would therefore be an unconscious mechanism aimed at creating cohesion in a group. It is above all a persuasive technique as it can create empathy and the emotional connection required for communication to be truly effective. This effect, in fact, can also be used in delicate situations to achieve the aim of creating connections and bonds: in this case imitating even in a very subtle way the way in which your interlocutor speaks, or gestures helps to arouse empathy and approval, always pushing him more towards our ideas.

Put it on speed when we talk

It's about being able to speak too quickly, even if it seems a little out of the box or even cringe! According to research conducted at the University of Georgia, however, the opposite was proven. According to research, when a person does not agree with our ideas, by speeding up our words and speaking very quickly, we give them less time to process the content of the speech and formulate an adequate cross-examination. Speaking quickly, therefore, can be a way to be prepared to break down the obstacles of those who are not like us and always bring them to our side. On the contrary, when you find yourself in front of a favorable audience, a slow and measured pace is advisable, which allows you to metabolize the message in its entirety.

The distraction technique

Think about when you are perfectly prepared and have clear ideas, whoever is in front of you perceives it and understands that it can be something to which it is impossible not to first pay attention and then say no. To make our communication even more effective, we can also take advantage of the opposite, that is, distraction. In fact, several studies have shown that when our public is tired and even more distracted, they become less inclined to send any requests back to the sender. Which simply means that he won't have the "strength" to rebel and say no!

Eyes fixed on the target

Another very effective persuasive communication technique was discovered in 2010 thanks to some researchers at the University of Newcastle. These researchers conducted a truly interesting experiment, in which a particular effect emerged: when they hung a poster depicting a large pair of eyes inviting people not to throw waste on the ground inside a bar, the customers felt even more obliged to throw their waste in the appropriate bins, rather than throwing it on the street or leaving it on the table. As if they felt watched! The hypothesis therefore emerged that ocular images could lead to more cooperative behavior, as they induce the idea of social control and therefore a sense of duty.

The confusion technique

In 1999, two researchers at the University of Arkansas first tested a persuasion technique that would later be called DTR (distract-then-restructure). To come up with such a strategy, they conducted an experiment in which they sold tickets for a charity raffle using a two-pronged approach. The first strategy was to sell potential customers 8 tickets for a total price of 3 dollars, while the second strategy aimed to offer a discount and sell the tickets (always 8) for 300 cents, pretending that they were a real deal. Despite the same price, the second strategy seemed to work wonders: sales, in fact, doubled. This is because a sort of disorientation was created, or better confusion, generated by the bizarre request, which made people, in a state of confusion, more inclined to accept the second strategy, seeing it as a pure and simple business. In essence, the DTR technique aims to confuse the routine of common thought, making the mind much more suggestible when faced with an apparently more advantageous alternative.

Select the best angle or viewpoint!

Another effective and persuasive communication strategy concerns a recent study carried out, in which it was demonstrated that, during a negotiation, the seller had to focus more on everything that the buyer could potentially gain from that specific sale, rather of what instead could represent a loss.
In short, it is about putting the issue in a different, better perspective, from an angle that increases the chances of having a concession and a positive response.

The strategy of tenacity and persistence

More than a technique, this should be a real rule: the moment we are coherent with our ideas, we master all the persuasive techniques in an equally coherent and impeccable way. It must also be said that, when we manage to demonstrate, in the long term, that we are willing to have the right degree of resilience and stubbornness, we almost always manage to get what we want. It's about always having a good dose of tenacity and persistence. With this we tell you to never be discouraged when faced with difficulties, but rather to try to take advantage of these difficulties and every obstacle that presents itself to acquire new experiences, knowledge and refine our persuasive and effective communication techniques.

Social Proof

When we talk about Social Proof, we refer to the credibility that is given to a thought or product thanks to the presence of a prominent personality, or simply following strong public approval. Approval and credibility are demonstrative elements, proving that this idea or product is socially accepted. If everyone recognizes and says that something is good for you or that it is useful and indispensable, then it will certainly be true.

This strategy, in other words, sets its effectiveness based on the public's uncertainty and personal fears. It is also a sort of imitation strategy, which occurs much more often than we think, in which people who do not know a topic well are unable to make decisions independently. In this case, they try to understand how others behave in the same situation to imitate their choices. Consequently, they take inspiration from the masses to direct their ideas and make them their own because they are commonly received by society, following, in a very instinctive way, a sense of identity and belonging. We feel part of a social group only when we share the same ideas and if we all act in the same way. In this way you will be able to sell your idea or product, since this idea is not only accepted by society, but is seen by many as an indispensable element of belonging.

Authority

Just as we talked about reciprocation and reciprocity as part of our educational background, respect for authority also represents one of the first lessons we receive from an early age. The concept of authority within a persuasive communication system can be a really fast and effective way to achieve our goal. It is a concept widely used in marketing and advertising, because the moment we recognize a person as an authority figure, we automatically accept his teachings or advice and are happy to obey his commands. Authority, in fact, confers preparation and competence in a certain field, giving us in return the security we need, for example, to purchase a certain product or medical aid. It becomes a pattern of unconscious choice, precisely because we believe it is right to obey and wrong to ignore the orders of a person of such prestige and competence. Let's see how we can instead become authoritative communicators and therefore worthy of people's listening and obedience. There are 3 tricks you can use:

1. The first measure, truly essential when it comes to becoming an authoritative person, is to work as hard as possible with tenacity and consistency (see the paragraph above). This gives us wisdom, awareness, preparation and competence, essential to be a leading figure.

2. Second trick: you must select an area and become an expert in that area, complete with qualifications and certifications. This will give you the knowledge and authority necessary to be recognized as people to listen to.

3. Third measure: it concerns the way in which we show our contents or the way in which we present ourselves and behave to you. In other words, the way we dress, pose and speak as we present our ideas can make a difference. An elegant and composed way of dressing and a way of presenting in a direct and imperative way gives a better response than someone who presents in an indirect, calm and polite way.

Make a great impression

In the field of sales, making an excellent impression is synonymous with a closed deal. In fact, there are several studies that demonstrate how, in the vast majority of times, people have met a friendly, affable seller and were so impressed and fascinated that they decided to purchase. What he liked, what gave them charm, were precisely their speeches and attitudes. Attitudes that make us feel appreciated and that create that sense of charm and security in every field of our lives! In the field of sales, in fact, almost each of us is more inclined to carry out actions that are requested of us by people we not only know, but who like us, like us and make us feel at ease. This type of affinity and liking can directly influence our choices even if the offers and products come from people we have never seen or known until that moment. Sympathy also leads us to trust people who give us positive feelings. Appreciation is one of the fundamental principles of persuasive communication, because it is very often based on the principle of reciprocity, which we mentioned at the beginning as one of the best strategies to follow. Likability, in fact, generates enthusiasm, which in turn is reciprocated with sudden gestures and actions without second thoughts, dictated precisely by the trust we are placing in that person.

Perceived value

Perceived value, as an effective and persuasive communication strategy, is understood as the difference between the benefits that would be obtained from a particular product and the effort required to obtain and take advantage of these benefits. In simple terms, it is about the perception of what positive things could be and what effort, what and how much work is needed to achieve it. Even if, at first glance and on paper, it might seem like an extremely objective evaluation, the perceived value can never represent the reality of the facts. The perceived value cannot be something universal, but becomes subjective and varies from person to person, based on different factors and elements characteristic of each of us. Let's take an example, a blue pen is objectively blue. But if that same pen is perceived by people with different shades of color from each other, then we will find ourselves in a situation where perception is dissonant with reality and therefore for some it is almost black, dark blue, light or purple. Precisely because of this subjectivity, when we have already managed to attract the public, who are interested in towards our speech or towards our product, we must be ready to show what we present in such a way that it demonstrates a high perceived value, complete with advantages and little effort to obtain them.

Perceived risk

After the perceived value, to develop excellent persuasive ability we need to know and apply the perceived risk technique. When we want to persuade a person, in this case, we will need to know very well what their resistances and defense weapons are, which very often are activated automatically: practically the famous obstacles! A very common example of resistance is the risk of losing money. This loss, here, represents the perceived risk which, based on this example, is directly linked to the amount of money that could be lost by concluding a bad deal. To remedy this, we can give, for example, a refund guarantee, or appeal to social proof, explaining that the product or our idea has already been tested several times and no one has ever complained or returned it (see how the various techniques are connected to each other)? Another element of perceived risk is also represented by the sphere of emotions. This risk factor manifests itself with a lot of doubts and objections in proportion to the importance given to the opinions of the people around us. Therefore, being able to understand the risk factors well and learn to manage them in every situation will help us to anticipate and resolve most of our interlocutor's objections, making our communication strong and unassailable.

Timing and contextualization

Contextualization and timing represent two essential strategic elements when it comes to persuasive and effective communication. Think about it: having the knowledge to propose an idea or a product at the right time and in the right context can be truly decisive for the success of our communication. Essentially being able to guess the exact moment is important in persuasive communication because it is the initial moment, that is, the moment in which we approach our interlocutor for the first time. To fully guess it, this moment must coincide with the exact moment in which that person is willing to listen to our words. It's also about understanding the propensity of our audience, whether they are ready or reluctant, and acting based on this understanding. The predisposition to listen increases more and more if, in addition to the timing, the context is also guessed. Therefore, knowing how to choose the right context and knowing how to intervene at a given moment is essential to obtain the desired result. And it makes us increasingly skilled and successful communicators (or sellers)!

Understand and exceed expectations

A very effective technique, from a persuasive point of view, is the one that concerns the expectations of our audience. Specifically, knowing how to understand the expectations of our interlocutor and making sure not to disappoint these expectations represents a decisive step towards effective and persuasive communication. Simply put, the persuasive skills that truly make our communication effective consist in understanding and therefore exceeding the expectations of others. The only variant is to take into account the fact that expectations are never fixed and objective ideas but vary from person to person and from case to case and can also be easily influenced; therefore, the strategy is never unique, but must be flexible and adaptable based on who is in front of us. Simply put, after having thoroughly studied what the expectations are, we must apply some sort of modeling process to these expectations so that our product, service or idea can easily exceed them and be sold in a certain way.

The dual Primacy and Recency Effect

The Primacy effect, the first of this technique, is the opinion that at first glance we all develop around a person, or a product or service. Therefore, it is based on the correct approach, as an incorrect presentation of the product can determine the failure of the entire persuasion process right from the start. The Primacy effect is therefore connected to the security we trust in ourselves and our ideas. If we are not absolutely convinced of our ideas and fail to make a good impression right away, we will hardly be able to change the minds and opinions of those who listen to us and bring them to our side. At this point, to succeed with the Primacy effect, we should focus on the initial part of our speech and prepare it in such a way as to fully capture people's interest, since they are the ones who instill a sense of trust and credibility towards us, the famous credibility that we have indicated as an essential strategy for being a good communicator. And here to maximize our chances of success it is essential to always be prepared. To be best prepared, we need to study our target audience even better than our product or service. To do this we can get to know our audience better on an emotional level have a well-structured speech, that is, one that follows previously established steps. In this case, improvisation is banned, even more so in the initial phase, precisely because it would highlight inadequate preparation which would compromise the rest of the transmission of our message.

Let's move on to the other effect, the Recency effect; with this term we refer to a sort of farewell, that is, the way in which we conclude our speech and say goodbye to our audience.

If the Primacy effect is relevant for giving a good overall impression and promoting the success of our speech, the Recency effect is the one that actually triggers a call to action. An example could be "leave us your email! And you will be contacted as soon as possible by our customer service." Once you have understood how to best conclude your persuasion process, you will then have to structure the rest of the speech, trying to emphasize the most relevant moments. To give a practical example, if we decide to end the speech with an invitation to perform a specific action, the main messages we want to focus on must be inserted, both at the beginning and at the end of the speech. And in this way the two effects match, making our persuasive communication strategy truly effective.

The urgency technique

The urgency strategy is a truly functional persuasive method because it boosts people's motivation to take immediate action. This urgency, precisely, is caused by the limited time available to them to decide. Generating a sense of urgency is crucial in communicative persuasion, since many people have a tendency to constantly procrastinate and, in this way, are instead pushed to make a decision as soon as possible.

The technique of truth

An effective strategy to immediately establish trust with our interlocutor is based on mere honesty. However, when we talk about truth, we are referring to a truth that few would have the courage to express. By exposing people to a harsh truth, the defense mechanisms of those in front of them crumble, allowing us to persuade them by offering our invaluable help, so necessary to face that harsh reality.

Behavioral flexibility

Having an extremely flexible mentality and knowing how to adapt to any circumstance is the key to successful persuasion. We have reiterated this several times. Mental flexibility becomes essential when applying persuasive communication in a group environment, especially when the number of listeners increases, increasing the likelihood of disagreements.

If we cannot manage the situation by ignoring some objections, it is advisable to abandon the discussion in the most effective way possible. However, if we manage to emerge victorious in a discussion with numerous objections, it is certainly thanks to our flexibility and ability to adapt.

To perfect this technique, it is essential to conduct a thorough study of possible objections. Knowing the possible objections in advance will allow us to adapt easily to various situations. By showing adaptability, keeping calm and remaining detached, we will in fact earn the maximum admiration from those who listen to us, since people tend to prefer those who manage their emotions wisely. Therefore, when you have to communicate, having an excellent ability to regulate your emotions is completely decisive.

Right framing technique

Framing is the process that induces individuals to interpret issues, events or realities in a varied way depending on how the information is presented to them.

As a result, the message recipient's perception of the information may change based on the frame provided for the content. The concept of framing, also known as the "framing effect", highlights the phenomenon whereby the same content, presented from different perspectives, can be interpreted in different ways by the interlocutor. When addressing a problem with different solutions, individual decisions can be influenced by the framing effect, which varies depending on how the content is presented, interpreted or organized in the discourse. This framing effect can exert a significant influence on persuasive communication and the way in which information is processed by the recipient of the message. From this there arise possible implications in the field of marketing.

In this chapter we have analyzed, studied in depth and shown in detail all the persuasive techniques that will then be useful in your private life and above all in your working life. We always want to remind you that to have good persuasive communication it is necessary to know as many techniques as possible to attract and keep the attention of our interlocutor, pique their curiosity and above all make them aware of our potential, recognizing us as authoritative and trustworthy people. Only thanks to the correct and consistent application of these techniques, would we have as many customers as possible willing to carry out the final act on our behalf.

It is always important to take into account the fact that all persuasion techniques play a fundamental role in our communication process, but they are of little use if those who apply them do not have the ability to exploit them or do not fully understand what they are for. It is therefore necessary to carry out a lot of study, do a lot of work and practice just as much exercise, but we are sure that you will soon master them perfectly.

Chapter 6: How to use correct tone of voice and fluency of speech

In this sixth chapter, we will close the part in which we talk about the techniques to apply for our effective and persuasive conversation with two fundamental elements which are the tone of voice and the fluidity of speech. Using these two elements, as we will see, allows us to improve and perfect our techniques, making our communication even more persuasive. Let's look at these two important factors in detail.

The general importance of tone of voice

Let's start by defining the tone of voice. With this expression we mean the whole set of those actions that have the aim of expressing the values, emotions, ethics and sensations of a message, giving it a specific intonation. In other words, tone of voice refers to not only the way we express our message through intonation but also the rhythm and emphasis we place on what we are communicating. The tone of voice is therefore the most concrete aspect of communication that we use every day. When we talk about a truly effective tone of voice, we are referring to a type of tone that has the purpose of conveying emotions with words, but also that of capturing attention and making your interlocutor live an emotional experience. It's a sort of performance: if you think about it, through the use of the right tone of voice the contents we are communicating can really take shape, at the same time expressing the personality of a brand or company. In addition to all this, the choice of the tone of our voice can modify the content and emotional impact of the communication itself. We talk about emotional impact precisely because each timbre of voice is different from the other, it expresses its own personality, its own rhythm; in short, it is a factor that distinguishes each of us and can really contribute to the success of our communication. This is because the tone of voice has a predominant influence on communication. It must also be said that, within the tone of voice itself, there are multiple sound parameters that attribute a conscious or unconscious meaning to the message we want to convey. To understand this difference in meanings let's take a small example: anyone can repeat the exact same sentence. However, it is precisely the tone of voice used that makes the difference, transmitting different psychological and emotional information. Even in words, therefore, there is a verbal and non-verbal content. And it is this last sphere which, being less controllable, is inevitably more authentic. And it makes us understand more about the person we are communicating with; we can precisely draw authentic psychological information about a person simply by analyzing their tone of voice. Even when different languages are spoken, thanks to the analysis of the tone of voice we could still understand a lot about that person, just by paying attention to how he speaks.

The advantages of a correct tone of voice

As we just said above, our voice and its use in a functional way represents a tool that is as wise as it is powerful. Knowing how to use the right tone of voice therefore brings a series of advantages. Great leaders are the first to understand that the tone of voice is everything. On the one hand it must be reassuring to gain the trust of their audience but on the other it must also be authoritative to give credibility to their message. In this case, credibility, authority and trust are some of the advantages of those who manage to use the right tone of voice in their communication. The correct tone of voice, as well as expressing good command of communication, can ensure that our message passes clearly and effectively. Knowing how to modulate our tone of voice also serves to give greater emphasis to our message, further capturing the attention of our audience. The tone of voice can also act as a guide to our audience: if we think about it carefully, even the very rhythm of communication (dictated by the tone of voice) can disorientate or, on the contrary, bring calm and self-control into a conversation. The mood and attention of our audience depend precisely on this.

The tone of voice also brings advantages when it comes to better regulating the collateral aspects of a conversation. On the one hand we are talking about paying greater attention to the volume to ensure that our words are understandable, on the other hand, the tone of voice also teaches us to know how to manage pauses and silences well to emphasize concepts.

The tone of voice brings benefits especially to the category of sellers, precisely because a sale is successful when a relationship of trust is established between seller and customer. In this case, active listening comes into play, but when the seller must respond and communicate empathetically with the customer, he must do so with a tone of voice that gives him an aura of trust, authority and reliability. It is not only necessary to be perfectly aware of the product we sell, but even more important is to be credible. And to do this, adjusting the right tone of voice, accent, rhythm and managing pauses become fundamental to succeeding in the sale.

How to create the right tone of voice

Now that we have understood both the importance and the advantages that the tone of voice brings to our communication, let's move on to practice with a step-by-step guide on how to create the correct tone of voice within our communication. The steps to follow will be those that we will indicate below:

1. As a first step to create the right tone of voice, an analysis must be carried out. An analysis in which we will understand who we are, our values and what we really want to convey. Simply put, it's about taking a journey of self-awareness to understand what distinguishes us, what we really want to achieve and start defining goals.

2. After understanding who we are, we should identify a set of words that fully represent us.

3. The third step, and now we are talking about a real tone of voice exercise, concerns the use of pronouns. Let's explain better: in this case the choice of pronoun influences the way in which our interlocutor sees us and therefore we must decide whether our tone of voice is aimed at the individual interlocutor or includes everyone. The use of "you" addressed to a single person shortens distances and involves the person, while addressing everyone with a general "you" puts everyone on the same level and makes you feel more part of a community.

4. Once the pronoun has been chosen, the other choice will fall on the language: should it be a formal language or a more colloquial one? In this case, to make your choice easier, you will have to ask yourself another question: what do we really want to communicate? But above all with whom? The use of formal language is particularly suitable for a body, an institution, or a bank. Having chosen the recipient and the formality of the message, our tone of voice must now be adjusted in order to convey professionalism, trust and authority. If the situation is more familiar and friendly, the language will become more informal making the conversation more engaging and fun.

5. The fifth step concerns the use of possible technicalities. Here too, the analysis will be aimed at the target audience. In most cases it is really not recommended to use overly technical terms because we refer you to a fundamental component of communication that must be clear and understandable. Too many technical terms only risk making communication too artificial, poorly constructed and not very fluid and force us to use a tone of voice that is often not suitable for us. The tone of voice must therefore be tuned to the "terms suitable for conversation" button!

The salient characteristics of the tone of voice in persuasive and effective communication

What are the characteristics that give us the best version of our tone of voice in effective and persuasive communication? Let's look at them in detail together:

✓ The tone of voice must be serious if the intention is to convey greater maturity and confidence in our audience; but if the tone of voice becomes very serious it alarms the public, alluding to something tragic or disastrous.

✓ The tone of voice with a strong and decisive connotation gives us importance and authority.

✓ A tone of voice that is too low can make our interlocutor understand that we have little self-esteem or are not fully aware of what we are communicating. It therefore becomes essential to adjust the tone of voice in order to communicate safety and trust in one's abilities.

✓ But in the same way, if the tone of voice becomes very high-pitched or shrill, it conveys little trust and little credibility in the public.

The hidden meanings in voice management: the importance of knowing how to recognize and use them best

At this point we can tell you that there are some truly precious hidden meanings behind managing the tone of voice suitable for effective and persuasive communication. Some psychologists revealed these secrets or meanings in voice management to us. These psychologists have managed, precisely, to collect a set of interpretations of numerous subtleties that we ourselves are often unable to even perceive and interpret. To help you communicate better and help you truly understand who is in front of you, here are all these meanings revealed.

Breathing

Let's start with breathing. Know that the way we breathe while speaking can provide an idea of the rhythm with which we approach life and with which, therefore, we communicate. Based on this assumption, we could say that the way we breathe communicates our current state of mind. Let's give some practical examples:

✓ Ways of breathing calmly: we transmit balance and serenity.

✓ Deep and constant: we transmit energy and dynamism.

✓ Deep, constant and strong: in this way we could communicate a state of repressed anger.

✓ Superficial: In this case, we may be communicating a lack of realism in our lives.

✓ Short and quick: in this way we can communicate a state of anxiety or distress.

Do you see how breathing is also important when it comes to communicating effectively and persuasively? Also regulating the breathing rhythm when communicating is essential to convey trust, balance and dynamism.

Intensity or volume

Regarding the intensity and volume of the tone of voice, we will show you the hidden meanings in general. These characteristics, in fact, define how a person interacts with himself and with others. So, if the volume is:

✓ Normal: we or our interlocutor want to convey self-control and listening skills.

✓ High: in this case more negative feelings such as weakness, selfishness and lack of patience are transmitted.

✓ Low: in this case, in addition to low self-esteem we could express inexperience and repression.

They had already said it above, but regulating our tone of voice to a normally acceptable volume is only synonymous with good communication and the transmission of positive feelings.

Articulation or vocalization

Vocalization or articulation of the voice are elements that have to do with the ability to understand and the interest in being understood. In this case if the vocalization is:

✓ Well defined: we will be able to convey mental clarity and openness to communication.

✓ Imprecise and hesitant: we could create a bit of mental confusion, appearing like someone who wants to deceive others.

✓ Very marked: too much is too much and, in this case, we could give the impression of narcissism, internal conflicts or tension.

✓ With hesitations: Here we can only convey aggression, insecurity or repression.

Remember that vocalization must always be well defined to convey not only safety but also trust in our listening audience.

Speed

Finally, we reveal the hidden meanings of the speed at which we communicate. The hidden meaning, in this case, coincides with the emotional moment in which the speaker is immersed, transmitting even more than we would like. If the speed of the tone of voice is:

✓ Slow: we may show disinterest and disconnection from the world.

✓ Quick: in this case tension, little preparation but also little desire to hide information could be the impressions we could give to our audience.

✓ Regular: in this case, moderation, naturalness and knowledge of speech are transmitted.

✓ Irregular: in this case we could transmit confusion, anxiety and a communication breakdown.

Speed is also an element that must always be taken into account when we want to convey our message in a clear, decisive and authoritative way. Therefore, carefully examine the hidden meanings behind our tone of voice and adjust them according to what you really want to convey.

The characteristics of the voice in non-verbal communication

We talked about the characteristics, advantages and hidden meanings of tone of voice in verbal communication. Let us now examine the salient aspects concerning of non-verbal communication. Vocal elements in a non-verbal context identify the quality of the voice and depend on social, biological and personality factors. The most striking example we can give you is to pay your attention to the tone of voice of a happy person and that of a sad, angry or disappointed person. In any case, all the transitory psychological factors that can influence the tone of voice in non-verbal communication are:

✓ Uncertainty

- ✓ Lie
- ✓ Seduction
- ✓ Irony or Sarcasm

Even silence, contrary to what one might commonly think, when inserted in the context of non-verbal communication, takes on an important meaning, especially when compared to different cultures. The meaning depends both on the character of the ongoing relationship and on the situation in which it is inserted.

The importance and interpretation of silence in non-verbal communication

Silence plays a fundamental role in our communication; did you know that? All great communicators understand the importance of silence and its skillful use to persuade those who listen to them. Silence, in fact, can actually express a set of meanings, even ambiguous or ambivalent ones. Above all, it transmits alternative meanings to our communication. What we mean is that it is rather simple to imagine situations in which, given the presence of emotional bonds between the interlocutors, even a brief silence in speech expresses immense feelings and meanings. For example, it can highlight agreement and sharing of ideas and feelings or, on the contrary, estrangement and disagreement. Silence can therefore convey consensus, but also disappointment (evaluative function). In other situations, silence can represent a pause for concentration and reflection, or on the contrary be a mental escape route and expression of distraction (activation function), or simply a way to take a breath and start the conversation again as best as possible. It can also have a function of omission or even disclosure of lies (disclosure function). If you think that silence represents a world of its own that does not respond to dictates or rules, you are very wrong: even silence has its rules and its interpretations. Understanding the importance and rules of silence together with language becomes fundamental when communicating in various environments, with various interlocutors and with different objectives. In most cases, silence is resorted to when relationships between individuals are still uncertain and insecure; that is, when there is little confidence between them. However, know that the rules of silence vary from culture to culture. In Western culture, prolonged silence during a conversation is usually interpreted negatively, as a loss of interest or willingness to deepen the mutual communicative relationship. In Eastern culture, on the contrary, it represents an element of intimacy and understanding, familiarity and even respect. The important thing is knowing how to use silence based on the context, our communication objectives, relationships with the public and, if it is a foreign public, applying it after having studied it in depth.

The other element: the fluidity of communication

Another fundamental element for communicating effectively and persuasively is represented by fluency. To understand fluidity, let's make a small premise that may seem trivial but is fundamental to better express the concept. Human beings, in general, constantly communicate with those around them, it is a real primary necessity! To do this they use different types of language. Now, one of the main types of communication is verbal language. Communicating orally and verbally and being able to do so in a clear, fluent and understandable way is something that is taken for granted, as if it were an innate gift, an ability already presents in most people, while not doing so implies a high level of limitation in our communication. Fluency therefore represents an inseparable element that we acquire over time and to ensure that our communication and our message reach the sender clearly and precisely. Fluency, in short, is the element needed to communicate better. In fact, let's face it, people who manage to communicate fluidly succeed in communicating better than others. It's not just about putting in the right information and words but pronouncing them in a certain way and with a certain emphasis allows them to perfectly convey a message or concept to their audience. At this point we can precisely define this concept: verbal fluency consists of the ability to maintain a dialogue in a clear and spontaneous way, managing to create connections between sentences and ideas in a natural and unforced way. Through verbal fluency, each speech becomes continuous and sustained over time, giving organicity and coherence to our communication (fundamental factors if we want to communicate effectively and persuasively). Communication with clarity and the right flow, in fact, will allow us to transmit ideas and information to our audience in an understandable way, with an adequate rhythm and avoiding unnecessary pauses and interruptions that could compromise understanding. In short, it also allows us to adjust our tone of voice in perfect harmony with what we are communicating. Poor verbal fluency and therefore poor clarity can derive from various causes, it can be a normal and intrinsic factor of the person himself, or of certain types of personal character, or of poor practice in the use of language, up to the presence of neurological disorders. As we have said, however, verbal fluency is not an innate ability but one that is perfectly trainable and acquirable. Below we will explain how.

How to improve verbal fluency

After understanding its meaning and importance, let's see what the best tips are for learning to manage and improve our verbal fluency. Below you will find, one by one, all these tips.

Expanding your vocabulary: the importance of increasing your reading

Reading is truly essential to enhance our ability to express ourselves easily. Above all, through reading, we will be able to expand our vocabulary, while also providing us with the linguistic tools necessary to converse in various professional and social contexts. The lack of verbal expression sometimes overcomes insecurity, which is linked to the lack of practical lexical skills, which can slow down the thinking process.

By possessing an extensive and varied vocabulary, we will therefore be better able to respond firmly and efficiently, avoiding ambiguity or verbosity.

Give strength to our words

To communicate persuasively, it is essential to enrich our language with a careful selection of words, stimulating a response from the interlocutor. To achieve success, we simply need to shape our statements around key terms or phrases. For example, if you want to persuade someone to buy car insurance, avoid mentioning only the number of accidents per day. Instead, emphasize the indispensability of insurance, highlighting the tragic number of deaths per day due to road accidents. Using stronger words, like "death," increases the persuasiveness of our message to the listener.

Let's express ourselves like our interlocutor

As mentioned previously, it is completely wrong to interrupt our interlocutor when he is expressing his needs and feelings. To choose the tone of your communication, carefully observe his verbal and behavioral style and adapt accordingly. It is a question, in other words, of being able to adapt our language to the level of the person we are interacting with: if he uses a common language, we should simply adapt our style, while if he uses a higher language, let's elevate ourselves too. Also always consider non-verbal communication: if your interlocutor gestures actively, imitate him by doing the same; if he is shyer, avoid gestures that might make him uncomfortable. Imitation, always if done in a very soft way, creates, as we have already reiterated in this guide, a climate of trust and collaboration that allows us to express our message at its best.

Avoid superfluous words and verbal fillers

Avoid inserting superfluous words, fillers or anything that could interrupt the fluidity of your speech. Every time we interrupt the flow or use excessive pauses, we inevitably decrease our credibility in the eyes of the interlocutor. The use of verbal fillers such as, "well", or "as I was saying" can compromise persuasive communication. In this regard, try to maintain clear and continuous communication, avoiding prolonged pauses and eliminating the excessive use of filler expressions. To improve, it is advisable to practice private speeches or think before you start speaking.

Tongue twister

Improving language fluency is achieved through exercise, which as we have already said, is a perfectly trainable skill. A very pleasant and practical way to hone this valuable skill is to use tongue twisters. Although they are very difficult for many, tongue twisters are a valid tool for completing sequences of similar words with few pauses, thus helping to perfect verbal skills. Green light to all the tongue twisters you know!

Theatricalization of scripts and role-playing games

An equally effective approach to developing verbal fluency is dramatization, which involves performing scripts or role-playing. To improve linguistic skills, it is necessary to perform publicly by narrating a text, reciting a short poem or reciting a sonnet previously studied and repeated.

Discuss topics over which you have perfect mastery

To speak correctly and fluently, we must be absolutely aware of what we are saying. It is a fundamental element, we have seen it several times, when seeking persuasive communication. Even if in everyday life the topics of conversation and what we communicate change depending on the topic of conversation or our interlocutors, it can be of great help to talk about topics about which we have a certain level of knowledge. To express ourselves with clarity and confidence, it is essential to address topics about which you have in-depth knowledge. Mastery of a topic promotes fluent communication, helping to develop confidence in your language skills.

Self-instructions out loud

To strengthen our communication skills and make them clearer and more fluid, it is beneficial to perform a physical action while explaining the actions and related steps aloud. This approach favors an improvement in communicative fluency, since concentration on the activity also contributes at an unconscious level.

Songs

An accessible and direct method to improve verbal fluency is singing, a trick within everyone's reach. Through the songs, you will replicate not only the sounds but also the tone of voice of the songwriters, helping to develop prolonged, fluid and clear speech.

These are all the tricks and tricks you will need to train and improve the fluidity of your conversation. Follow them with care and consistency and you will see that the results will not be long in coming! In this chapter we analyzed the importance of tone of voice and linguistic fluency in persuasive communication. We also explained how the tone of voice is fundamental as this vehicle allows us to express values, emotions, ethics and sensations.

Our tone of voice, used wisely and correctly, also serves to transform verbal and non-verbal language into words and emotions and to persuade the people who listen to us, touching their most intimate and deepest chords. Furthermore, once we understand the importance of tone of voice and how to interpret various tones of voice, we will also be better able to practice active listening and understand what our audience really wants. If we then want to become truly successful communicators, we will have to learn to modulate our tone of voice and use it not only to express emotions but also to repress them when the context is the wrong one. A separate paragraph has been dedicated to a fundamental aspect of non-verbal speech, the importance of silence in communication. Silence, as we have seen, is capable of taking on a set of alternative meanings, such as expressing assent or dissent within the same social group. We also underlined the cultural connotation and then moved on, in the second part of the chapter, to talk about another fundamental element, namely the so-called fluidity of communication. We have understood its absolute importance, that it is not an innate ability but that, thanks to the right tools such as those provided in the last part, we can train to improve the fluidity of our communication. Having concluded this part, in the next part it will be explained to you, again in practice, how to apply persuasive and effective communication techniques based on the various contexts that arise from time to time.

PART FOUR - THE APPLICATION OF EFFECTIVE AND PERSUASIVE COMMUNICATION IN VARIOUS CONTEXTS

This fourth part will be dedicated to the various situations that can be shown to us on a daily basis. Here, now our aim is to ensure that, on a communicative level, you can always get by great, pursuing your individual objectives. The next chapter, in fact, will show the different communication approaches with various examples and specific situations. A part relating to the working context and how to approach communication with your employees will also be presented. The eighth chapter will instead focus on practical examples of everyday life in which you can apply these different communication approaches.

Chapter 7: The different approaches depending on the specific situation and examples

We have seen so far that persuasive and effective communication is the linguistic, verbal and non-verbal ability to be able to tune in perfectly with one's interlocutor; it is also a question of being able to transmit certain messages to him, based on his frequency of perception. This small summary, applied to any context of daily life, makes us understand that to achieve persuasive and effective communication it is necessary to act first of all on the unconscious of one's interlocutor: the vast majority of the work of persuasive communication is therefore carried out at an unconscious level. Once this has been established, it will be much easier for you to understand that you will have achieved perfect harmony with your interlocutor only when you are able to communicate directly with his unconscious. Our way of communicating with others, in fact, has a decisive impact on people who will feel emotionally involved in the relationship. This way of communicating becomes effective through the propensity of our interlocutor to interact with us on a continuous basis, both in informal and work contexts. In this seventh chapter, in fact, we will analyze all the various cases of persuasive and effective communication applicable in different fields and with different types of people, using a linguistic register appropriate to the situation.

Again, to make things easier for you, you will also be shown examples that can be applied in various situations. Let's start!

The communication linguistic registers

The first thing to do to become a master's in communication in various situations is to understand the existence of the various linguistic registers. Knowing the different linguistic registers means understanding the styles and choices that are usually used in the various contexts. The linguistic registers used in communication, in fact, are nothing more than the set of expressive choices used in different communicative contexts. Each linguistic register is therefore characterized by the syntactic, morphological and lexical choices made. Linguistic registers depend above all on the context and status of our interlocutor. Taking a practical example, with our boss we will never use the same linguistic register used for example with our acquaintances or relatives. That said, below we will show you five basic types of linguistic registers:

Courtly or wanted register

This first type of register will be applied to particularly esteemed interlocutors who are required to have a deferential and respectful attitude. A more refined register, in fact, will be entirely concentrated on the use of particular words suited to the highest context of conversation, cultured quotations, and highly studied and richly elaborated syntax. This type of register of facts will be used in situations in which characters interact, particularly those who are cultured or belonging to a high social class. To give a practical example, it is the register that is used above all in conferences and other scientific occasions, such as official meetings between ministers or members of a delegation. The lexicon is based on refined, elegant, respectful expressions; the period instead is varied, broad, with the use of subordinate clauses.

Bureaucratic register

If we wanted to think about the type of register used in various office situations, it would be the bureaucratic register. In this case, in fact, a rigidly impersonal and anonymous approach is usually required, where the vocabulary is studied but sober, without refinement. At the same time, the syntax is elegant but without excess and the tone is technical-administrative. The bureaucratic register, therefore, is mainly used in writings in which a public body or a person is addressed in the context of their specific professional role.

The learned register

The learned register is applied between interlocutors who do not have real acquaintance relationships. It is therefore applied in exchanges of a professional nature, as happens in conferences or in official declarations. The form is correct and accurate; the syntactic construction adequately elaborated; appropriate lexical choices, and sometimes there is a certain refinement.

Medium register

The medium register is the one used every day in social and professional relationships. It can also be said that it is applied in interpersonal relationships of a not strictly confidential type, in which the lexical choice is precise but not particularly accurate. In this type of register there is no slang, but the syntax remains correct, although it is not given the typical elegance of the courtly register. It is, in fact, the linguistic variety most used verbally or in writing, in mass communications, in radio and television news, in newspapers, in information texts in general, in schoolbooks; the syntactic structure is flat and flowing; the appropriate vocabulary, free of dialects, slang as we said above and colloquialisms.

The colloquial register

Finally, we see the register being applied in private contexts and in more informal communicative exchanges. The colloquial register is in fact the one you use with your family, friends or people with whom you are very familiar. Here the lexical choices used can be generic, the syntax is simplified or typical of speech and sometimes of slang or dialect expressions.

The syntactic construction is not very articulated and refined; the vocabulary, simple and not very refined, gives ample space to regionalisms and colloquial terms and idioms with a certain expressive connotation. It's basically what we also use in messaging.

The 3 rules of the most effective conversation

Did you want the secret to have the best conversations revealed? Here it is: to be one of those people with whom it is always pleasant to talk and who is therefore appreciated by others and sought after, the only secret is to talk with others, not through others or for others. You must be the direct communicator and no one else. To do this, you need to apply the right words to the context (the famous registers indicated above). Having made this choice, we must also always be perfectly aware of the words we pronounce, without throwing words out there at random. In fact, those in front of us react to the words we say. Often, in fact, the people we are communicating with can be sensitive to certain subtle allusions in our statements, which is why we must always have a clear identikit of the person we are communicating with. In this regard, in addition to the correct choice of register, the secret is to embrace the 3 fundamental rules of effective communication. In fact, according to Dr. Karl Albrecht, an expert in communication and leadership, the secret to being a good conversationalist is to monitor and balance three elements of communication: declaratives, questions and conditionals. Let's see specifically what it is.

Declarative expressions

Declarative expressions refer to statements about facts, or at least about something we know for certain to be a fact that actually exists. Declarative expressions are, therefore, a mere statement of a speech that is evident in the facts, and that can be confirmed with a lot of evidence. Be careful, many false statements are sometimes passed off as real, disguised as apparently tangible evidence. You will have to make sure, in this case, to start a conversation with statements that are almost exclusively declarative, with effective evidence, but above all free of personal opinions.

Requests

The other rule specifically concerns questions. Thanks to questions it is possible to allow others to contribute to our communication with what they know and think they know. In addition to this, questions give a personalized tone to the conversation and allow others to feel that they are actively participating in the conversation rather than passively subjected to it.

To make questions the golden rule of super-effective communication, ask a discreet number of them during a conversation, without exaggerating so as not to seem inappropriate. The right questions must be asked especially when we are in front of a large audience, to demonstrate that we are willing to share the scene with those who are listening to us. Let's also make sure to ask your questions in a curious but delicate way, without slipping into interrogation, as we said above, trying to respect the level of openness that our interlocutor is willing to grant us.

Conditionals

Conditionals, also known as "qualifiers," are polite ways of expressing our views, opinions and perspectives, while recognizing that others, despite what we say, have the right to see things differently. different than us.

For this reason, using expressions such as "It seems to me that", "According to my experience", "I'm not entirely sure", makes us more aware of our respect towards others, who will also feel they have the full right to express a point of a different point of view than ours. In practice, although we may find ourselves disagreeing with our interlocutor and not sharing his point of view, we point out our respect for what he is expressing. However, not everyone understands the importance of this step. People who are not very assertive and who show considerable difficulty in asserting their opinions may reject this conversational strategy, considering it weak or a waste of time. These people are strongly frightened by the fact of finding themselves in front of another person with a different vision from theirs, so it is up to us to put these people at ease by placing ourselves in the conditional rather than the imperative.

Making these people feel respected and welcome is one of the secrets that leads us to have a more involved audience that is more inclined towards our goals.

Let's put the 3 secrets rule into practice

To evaluate the full effectiveness of the "rule of the three secrets of effective communication", you can do the following exercise for several days. When you are engaged in a conversation, be it informal or formal, monitor, first of all, the percentage of declarative expressions, then the interrogatives and conditionals that you will use. Monitoring serves to understand our usual style. From this examination, can it be seen whether we only use declarations complete with verifiable facts? Do we ask enough questions so that our interlocutor can also express themselves? If so, does your way of asking questions denote respectful curiosity or is it more like a fairly ambiguous interrogation? Do you use the conditional when you express yourself, or do you usually use dogmatic expressions that leave no room for opinions different from yours? Take this exam and understand if the 3 secrets rule is balanced or is more focused on questions, statements or conditionals.

Perhaps we didn't underline it enough above, but overall, a proper conversation should include all three types of communication, which alternately intertwine with the expressions of one's interlocutors; but above all that they balance perfectly. Now, to put them into practice in an exemplary way, after a few declarative sentences, try to start the conversation by asking a question, so that the other person can also start interacting with the conversation and also formulate their own question, always relevant to the speech. When you go to answer, try to insert a conditional answer to make it clear in a very respectful way that, although the opinion may differ from yours, it will not only not be ignored, but will be taken with due consideration. At this point, the conditional, and this is what it is for, allows us to consciously reorganize our conversation. Thanks to this pause, we can try to detect the reactions, even the most subtle, shown by others and try to understand if the rule of 3 allows us to create more empathy, precisely that empathy that serves not only to have more rewarding but also persuasive conversations. So, during a conversation, especially monitor the proportion of the three types of expressions you use. Above all, try to understand what type of influence the prevalence of each of the three expressive modes has on your ways of communicating and on you.

Now that we have discovered the secrets of communication in practice, let's now analyze specific cases, and in particular within a team.

How to communicate effectively within our team

Let's take one of the most practical examples regarding effective and persuasive communication: let's put our position as leaders within a work context. We will certainly have a team available. Teams with which we should necessarily communicate; but how can we improve communication in our team, so as to make everyone feel involved and listened to and perhaps inclined towards our proposals and objectives? To this end, this paragraph will show you how to always have professional and intelligent conversations with our employees or collaborators. To do this, we chose the method invented by Sarah Harvey, an English communication expert. This model of effective communication serves to improve conversations between colleagues and was the result of study and application in practice, in which effective conversations were held in the workplace, made with intelligence, clarity, which get to the point, and which do not create tension or conflicts between the various participants. The model we are talking about is called STREET CREDS. The two terms are nothing more than the union of the acronym of the 6 principles that inspire it and its 5 essential ingredients. So, let's examine them in detail.

The 6 principles on which the model is based are those of the acronym STREET and are as follows:

Safety

The first term refers to safety: in this case it translates into making sure that all the people involved in the conversation feel safe. In other words, it's about putting your team at ease, where each participant feels at ease within themselves, without the fear of someone asking them embarrassing questions. Or an aggressive or irritating approach is used that puts pressure on others and pushes them to deviate from our goals.

Trust

Trust is also very important in this communication model. In fact, if we want conversations to flow easily and be open and sincere, the first thing we should do is to create trust within the team. In fact, if trust is lacking, communication cannot be at a good level. Building trust requires patience and taking the time to get people to know and trust each other.

Reason

Pattern also plays a vital role in this pattern. Think about it: if your goal is to establish an effective conversation, you will have to be perfectly aware of the reasons that drive you, the real ones obviously. Know that, in everyday life, the best reasons to start a conversation within a team are to solve a problem or get approval for a project or goal. So be perfectly aware of why you want to start this conversation. Improvising is never the right solution, especially if you have people who depend on your leadership.

Emotions

The emotional sphere and its regulation, as we have already explained to you, have enormous relevance when it comes to managing an effective conversation. Now, ask yourself the following question: Are we able to manage our emotions when we participate in a conversation? Or are we always able to identify the type of emotion and make sure that they do not compromise the outcome of the discussion, but above all that they are not a type of emotion that does not harm you or others? Within the team it is about managing emotions in a two-way way. So, try to control your emotions and invite others the need to do so. Emotional intelligence is very useful for this purpose, thanks to which it is possible to have more effective and pleasant conversations.

Exchange

Being able to have an exchange is the fundamental ingredient in a conversation within a team. This is because, being able to have a respectful exchange of ideas, above all has an impact on the type of relationships we have with our team. The exchange, therefore, excludes all elements to avoid a conflictual relationship and promote a more collaborative climate.

Truth

For many, the truth may indeed seem uncomfortable, but sometimes it is necessary if we want to have more honest and fruitful conversations. Sincerity, in fact, is much more useful when it comes to solving problems, facing challenges and achieving the goals we have set.

Once we have learned and applied the six principles of effective conversation, we can put them into practice by verifying that these six elements interact with each other and positively influence each other. Therefore, keep in mind that if one of these elements is missing, there will most likely be a strong imbalance and the climate within our team will be much more negative and less inclined to seek appropriate solutions. It is equally important to also balance the other five elements related to the CREDS acronym. Let's look at them better below:

Candid

When dealing with difficult or delicate topics in particular, the conversation should be candid, in the sense that, connected to the element of truth indicated above, it must be real and frank. Therefore, any hypocrisy or other behavior that could ruin the conversation and lower the level of trust is banned. Being candid also means getting to the point: there's no point beating around the bush when we have to say something very uncomfortable. In other words, we always try to be clear and state things as they are without ambiguity. For example, if within the team there is a person whose work is of an unsatisfactory quantitative or qualitative level, the issue must be addressed openly, without creating tension and embarrassment.

Respectful

Connecting to what we have just said, even if our conversation must be open, candid, frank and direct, we still need to be careful to use the right methods. This is where respect comes into play: therefore, avoid using aggressive or accusatory tones but talk about the problem with the person concerned, without making them feel uncomfortable. Always show him courtesy, politeness and respect. Show him consideration and, before addressing the critical points to improve, praise the part of the work he carries out with care and professionalism.

Engaging

To be truly effective within our team, a conversation must be professional, useful, respectful and interesting for everyone. However, it must also be engaging to ensure that it arouses real interest and participation from everyone. It is therefore necessary to try to create involvement and participation in the conversation. No monologues, but let the others speak and participate too. In this case, the precious active listening that we have talked about several times comes into play. As we listen, let us always remember to show interest in the arguments of others. Once this is done, we make our team members understand that the improvements that, for example, we are requesting are in the best interest of the team as a whole. We also remind you that it is always essential to create a climate of trust and positive collaboration if we want people to speak openly and without fear.

Direction

Taking the conversation in the right direction means getting to the point quickly without rambling, wasting time or procrastinating. To do this, we should always keep ourselves focused on the objective we want to achieve, and on the appropriate path to follow to solve the present problems. Problems that actually slow down or hinder the path and achievement of the set objectives. In this regard, the focus should be on problem-solving actions and not on looking for every possible culprit.

Sensitivity

Above, the full relevance of getting to the point and staying focused on the objectives was emphasized. However, tact is always needed: in other words, we need to consider the situation and the moment that each member is experiencing within our conversation. The right sensitivity takes into account, for example, the privacy of team members. It's also about being tactful in assessing whether it's the most appropriate moment or not: for example, it's useless to burden the same person with the task of solving that problem if they're already dealing with other big problems and it's impossible for them to manage everything together. It is also important to know how to manage the emotions and reactions that our interlocutor may have. Empathy always comes into play here, which we now know is the essential ingredient of effective and persuasive communication.

Our seventh chapter also ends with these elements, shown one by one.
This chapter has illustrated various situations in which persuasive communication can be applied, with examples of standard communication suitable for specific contexts. To learn how to manage different conversations in various contexts, we have illustrated the concept of linguistic register. This refers to the expressive choices used in various communicative situations and includes five types of register: courtly or refined, bureaucratic, learned, medium and colloquial. Furthermore, the rule of 3 was presented, which concerns the use of declarative expressions, questions and conditionals. In the next article we will look closely at some practical examples of effective communication in daily life.

Chapter 8: Some practical examples of daily life and advice on work

Here we are at the eighth chapter of this practical guide on effective and persuasive communication. In this part we will take care not only of providing you with some practical examples, but also of providing invaluable advice to help you become true communication experts. These tips and practical examples are particularly aimed at the world of work. Here you will learn to communicate correctly whether you are in the command position or in a subordinate position.

Some examples and practical advice for communicating with your employees every day

After having discussed at length the rules and secrets for correct, effective and persuasive communication, even with your collaborators within a team, let's now see what the practical examples are on how to apply this type of communication. If you want to truly communicate with your employees every day, all you have to do is:

✓ First of all, create a fast line of communication that is based on everyday life. What we are trying to tell you is that communicating does not just mean talking: in this case it could also mean organizing an email calendar updated every day; it could also mean spreading the company culture through, for example, a newsletter focused from time to time on a specific theme or on a fragment of its company code, trying to be engaging, asking for answers and encouraging staff participation. This serves to increase the famous engagement and ensure that our employees become the first supporters of the company.

✓ To not only give orders to our staff but also create a climate of sharing, in which we instill our knowledge in our collaborators, aiming for the growth of each of them. In this way, it will be possible for us to create a virtuous circle which will also allow us to retain all possible talent and reduce staff turnover.

✓ Pay our attention to semantics and use a communication code consistent with company values. In other words, the choice of our words must be consistent with our behaviors. Communicating effectively with staff also means knowing how to spread the right values and corporate culture.

✓ Highlight and trace the path of information, analyzing the critical points of communication, resolving them and creating company protocols, also in this area. Communicating poorly with employees, perhaps you don't know it yet, represents a cost and a negative point for our company. There are many entrepreneurs who make the big mistake of neglecting the dialogue with their employees, which, if it is not transparent and clear, does not allow us to involve staff in the problem-solving process, nor to share and achieve objectives together.

✓ Use, thanks to social media and new technologies, effective communication also to do team building and create involvement. You can think, for example, of company contests in which employees' ideas are listened to, or of virtual spaces in which to meet and share one's passions, exchange information in order to create osmosis between work and personal life.

Establish effective and persuasive communication with our boss

Now let's think about the case in which we were on the opposite side, and we were the employees. In this case, we should be good at communicating with our boss, trying to make him understand how we feel and what can be useful to help him manage problems in a more effective and satisfying way. Life as an employee, like that of a leader, is not always all roses and flowers. To the detriment of those who find themselves in a subordinate position, they often have to deal with bosses who, rather than collaborating, prefer to instill fear or make employees uncomfortable. Let's be clear, not everyone knows how to be a leader, in fact many prefer to just be "bosses" who give orders, totally ignoring the effective communication advice just given above. Apart from this, for our part, we can never take for granted that our boss is able to read our minds and therefore has the responsibility to know how we feel or what exactly to say to improve our situation. We must always be perfectly aware that he or she is not someone who knows us in depth or hangs out with us all the time; therefore, he could often make mistakes when approaching his employees. Having said that, we are the ones who have to communicate and explain to him how to best manage our feelings, for example by explaining to him what could be motivating or demotivating within that specific company so that the work can be done in the best possible way. To communicate in a functional way, we should explain to our boss what we actually need, what we want to improve without however expecting to always be 100% understood. We are obviously aware of the fact that talking about our feelings to the boss can be difficult, but the discussion, if conducted clearly, effectively and persuasively, it could also lead to a better relationship with him or her.

Here's how it might be possible to establish a type of efficient communication with our superior at work:

✓ First of all, before starting any type of communication, we need to be completely honest and understand if what we want to achieve is really suitable for us, or simply if we deserve it. We are sure that we are ready or deserving of a promotion or management of an important project or appreciation for our work. Or again, are we ready to have greater inclusion in decision-making power, in control over an activity? Are we able to be seen from a future growth perspective? Or do we really need greater clarity, respect, autonomy?

- ✓ Having asked these questions, we can now really understand what we want to ask or communicate to our boss.
- ✓ Establish the requests, decide on a time and place to meet your boss, so that we are perfectly ready to start our communication.
- ✓ Once met, it will be a matter of describing, always in a very clear and concise way, what we believe happened, where there were shortcomings, and what we think we deserve at this moment. If it is a question of describing a certain event, try to describe very briefly the part that influenced you negatively. It is also a matter of speaking in a very general way, without ever going into detail. So describe in a very simple way, for example, how you were interrupted during a conversation, a decision that made you feel uncomfortable, or the reasons why you were not considered for a project, a decision, a promotion, etc..
- ✓ Describe, always in a very clear and concise way, the impact that the event had on you. This is the essential moment to clearly express who we are, what emotion we felt and above all why that particular behavior made us feel this way (so that it is not repeated in the future).
- ✓ So, the time has come to tell our boss what we really need. What do we expect from the boss in the future? It's about starting to make small requests, which must be clear and short.
- ✓ The time has come to pass the ball to our boss, and above all give him the time necessary to respond to our requests. Here, to ensure that our communication has truly been effective, we must never become defensive. Now, we must remain calm and be patient. We have already expressed our requests, needs and conditions, so we don't have to do anything anymore. Now the word goes directly to the boss. It could also happen that the boss reacted badly at the beginning, but by giving him enough time to reflect, it is very likely that his response will soon be positive.
- ✓ Avoid clashes: it's about not using conflict strategy to pursue your desires but focusing on collaboration and trying to understand your boss's point of view to address the situation together.
- ✓ We replace the "but" with "we believe": if our boss proposes an approach different from the usual one, we avoid using abrupt and personal answers, replacing with "I think" to express our opinion, for example, "I think we could obtain better results this way."

What to avoid saying to our boss

We looked at how to communicate our dissatisfaction and feelings to our boss. To conclude this discussion, it is important to highlight what is best to avoid expressing to your supervisor. For example, you should avoid directly reporting an employer's mistake, as this could suggest a challenge to authority. Instead, it is preferable to address the issue tactfully, perhaps hinting at a misunderstanding in communication.

Furthermore, it is advisable to refrain from complaining directly and aggressively about a colleague, for example, avoiding starting the conversation with phrases such as "Did you see what he did yesterday?". It is preferable to address issues of this kind in a formal way, avoiding information or chatter, and to do so only when a colleague actually violates the rules. Finally, it is not recommended to try to "blackmail" the employer by means of ultimatums without alternatives, such as for example by saying " either you do this, or I leave". The results could be extremely negative.

How to set up convincing conversations to impress your superior

After examining effective communication strategies with your boss, we will now give you some practical advice on how to conduct conversations that leave a positive impression. It's essentially about asking targeted questions to get attention without appearing arrogant. Better questions might be:

✓ First, "How are you?" Our manager may be under pressure, and a question like this gives him pause to think. The answer doesn't matter, but the gesture of asking is still of fundamental importance.

✓ "Can I help you with anything?" It facilitates the delegation of tasks and demonstrates our willingness and motivation to contribute.

✓ "Are there any important people to meet?" When starting a new job, it's critical to gain a comprehensive understanding of the organization by talking to other teams or executives. Asking will demonstrate our willingness to take the initiative without seeming pushy.

✓ "What are the goals for next year?" Showing long-term interest will give the impression of commitment from day one, especially significant if we are among the new recruits. Alternatively, we can simply ask what their goals are for next year.

✓ "Do you have any tips to share?" Remaining generic and showing your willingness to accept feedback, including critical feedback, is important to make people understand the importance of the boss's position within the company. This question offers an opportunity to understand the boss's thinking and priorities.

✓ "What is his favorite method of communication?" Given the intense activities, understanding how to maintain adequate information exchange is crucial. Some prefer direct dialogue, others prefer communication via email or telephone. Establishing the foundation for effective communication is essential from the beginning.

How to achieve effective and persuasive communication during a job interview

Meeting someone for the first time, especially in an interview setting, can generate tension. This anxiety is increasingly common, especially in the workplace. During an interview, the goal of our communication is to make a quick impression without being overwhelmed by anxiety. At the same time, it is essential to show interest in the interlocutor without falling into a position of psychological inferiority. Communication is crucial to successfully managing an interview; therefore, it is essential to adopt a positive attitude. Obviously, courtesy and friendliness are key elements in conducting the interview, but at the same time it is important to express your opinions freely. Interviewers appreciate those who can take a stand and explain their motivations. It is also essential to convey reliability through appropriate language and the right non-verbal language, while the ability to listen carefully allows you to intervene in a relevant way. This approach will allow us to showcase our best qualities.

The fundamental rule for leaving a good impression is to be authentic, avoiding exaggerating with skills you don't possess. Being yourself promotes a more comfortable environment during the interview. Recruiters are experts at detecting a lack of sincerity and look for authenticity in the people they place with companies.

Therefore, when preparing for an interview, we need to think carefully about ourselves, identifying our strengths and weaknesses, and using them to our advantage. It also serves to transform any gaps into opportunities for growth and improvement to make us more "attractive" to those who hire us.

Practical advice and tips on how to communicate effectively and persuasively in a job interview

Typically, recruiters conduct interviews for multiple positions at the same time. When dealing with many people during these meetings, it is essential to pre-select and identify three or four candidates for a second interview.

Let us therefore remember that, in addition to us, there will probably be ten other people to be examined on that day. The main goal is to make sure that recruiters remember us at the end of the day and have made a great impression. They will remember us for the words spoken or the attitude adopted; otherwise we will be forgotten as soon as we leave the office. To achieve our objectives through persuasive and effective communication, it is essential to follow some rules and advice such as those we will show you below.

Stay focused during the conversation

Maintain focus during the conversation, something that can easily get out of hand. Imagine a recruiter interviewing several people and being faced with someone who is distracted or has a short attention span. In such situations, the interview is likely to end with the usual "we'll let you know" phrase and a goodbye.

A helpful tip is to turn off your phone before your appointment or put it on night or silent mode. An additional tip in these situations is to maintain eye contact with the recruiter. This will help avoid distractions caused by background noise, such as traffic or sounds from the next room. It will also help you avoid getting distracted by gestures like someone playing with a pen while they're talking to you.

Stay active

Showing dynamism is another quality you should highlight during the job interview. This doesn't involve asking casual questions in an exaggerated or ostentatious way, but rather clearly demonstrating that you're following the conversation carefully. In other words, if during the conversation with the recruiter we are not able to keep our gaze fixed, and perhaps we will stare at the ground due to shyness (or, even worse, we will stare into space) and we do not actively participate, we will seriously risk transmitting disinterest in the job position.

Adopt a more formal tone to maintain professional behavior

Highlighting our skills and past experiences is essential for our job interview, always trying to maintain a certain distance and respect.

Remember that our interlocutor is not a relative, but a potential employer. An overly friendly tone, especially in the first few minutes, may not always be well received. Therefore, avoid jokes, since, although they may arouse laughter, in some cases they could be interpreted as arrogance or presumption. Also eliminate sarcastic phrases from your language, as they are often not understood, especially by those who don't know you, and could take on different meanings from those we intended.

References

Having good references, in addition to being synonymous with great professionalism, gives considerable added value to the interview.

Talk and warm up your voice, take a walk to focus on the key points of the interview and clear your head. What you will focus your references on will be your academic background, first job, career breakthrough and current position.

Salary negotiation

Navigating the salary discussion is a challenge. Furthermore, there are three key elements to consider in this context:

1. Expectations: What is the market value of my role, in line with the company where I am interviewing.
2. Optimism: What amount represents a significant improvement over my current salary and will fully satisfy the financial proposition?

3. Review your options: What is the minimum offer that would make us seriously consider a career change?

Some examples of effective conversations during a job interview

After having shown you how to manage the job interview profitably, here are some practical conversation examples to help you stand out from other candidates and continually be taken seriously. To set up an effective conversation, after the interviewers have asked you questions to understand aspects of your professional experience and the quality of your skills, it will now be our turn to ask questions. However, it is necessary to ask the right questions. For example, we could ask:

✓ What are the key factors for excelling in this position? Does the company intend to make a new hire and is looking for a professional capable of contributing to the company's operations? Requesting information on performance indicators (KPIs) demonstrates a strong commitment to growing professionally and providing value to the organization.

✓ Does my experience fit the profile the company is looking for? Expressing an interest in a subjective opinion highlights a willingness to receive constructive feedback, since it is usually up to the interviewer to provide evaluations. Understanding the company's opinion can help you build rapport and ask intelligent questions during the interview, while also demonstrating a serious commitment to the role.

✓ What are the main challenges associated with this position? This question, while intimidating, offers numerous benefits. The response, if clear, immediate and positive with explanations, indicates a positive signal; on the contrary, hesitations could be alarming bells. In this context, it is not the interviewer who evaluates us, but we are evaluating the company. Informed candidates are those, in fact, those who wish to understand the challenges associated with the role.

✓ What results does the company expect from my position? This question highlights our predisposition to anticipate and solve challenges. The answer can clarify the reason for the position opening, providing guidance for success. By showing ourselves as potential team members, we demonstrate that we want to contribute to the achievement of excellence by all our colleagues.

✓ Are there any changes compared to previous procedures? This question is directly linked to the previous one and allows you to understand if the employer is looking for new skills to complete the work process and needs changes to improve its quality.

✓ What is your typical daily work routine? This question aims to explore the practical organization of work in detail. The interviewer can provide information about workloads, daily activities and additional responsibilities. Furthermore, asking if there are changes compared to previous procedures links directly to this question, allowing you to understand if the company is looking for new skills to optimize the work process or improve quality.

✓ What is the training program related to the work process? Basically, you are trying to understand the procedures and resources that will be used to facilitate your autonomy and adaptation to the dynamics of the job. The response should be clear and detailed, providing information on timing and evaluation criteria during the induction period.

✓ Is there a continuous development program? This question aims to evaluate the importance of continuous training within the company culture. While we may initially take on an entry-level role, having relevant specialist courses may present an opportunity to enhance our skills and progress professionally.

✓ How are internal progression levels managed? It is essential to be aware of the methods by which employee merit is recognized and what criteria define advancement. Promotion possibilities and the average time to reach them offer concrete information on growth prospects within the company.

Speaking in public: how to get by in this case too

Many mistakenly believe that public speaking is an innate rather than an acquired ability, or in any case that it is simply a personal predisposition. In reality this is not the case. We can all become good public speakers and develop great public speaking skills. It is therefore possible to work to improve our communication in front of more people: in fact, there are strategies, tricks, techniques and exercises for speaking in public.

Until now, in fact, communication has been set up, with practical examples, when speaking with a single person or a small circle. Now we will explain how to address a wider audience, without anxieties and fears. To ensure that our communication is truly effective in this case too, we must, first of all, know our audience well. It is therefore a question of studying in depth the doubts of those in front of us, their uncertainties, and above all their language. Having said this, it is right that we now dedicate some of our attention to the importance of speaking in public. How important is it to do it well? It is really important because, being able to speak efficiently even in front of many people offers many opportunities. Already think about job opportunities. There are many job positions where good public speaking skills are required. Even within our job itself, speaking and presenting well in public can really offer us the chance to advance our careers. In essence, becoming a good public speaker can on the one hand increase our self-confidence, but on the other it can increase our reputation within the work environment and perhaps lead to new opportunities. Developing these good communication skills in public, in fact, can open many doors for us, poor skills in this field can close them. To make you understand even better the importance of having good communication skills in public, let's give you a small example: assume that you should convince potential customers to buy during a sales presentation. If you fail to convey and communicate the value of that particular product well, you could lose valuable contracts, denying yourself not only the possibility of earning money but also of being able to positively impress your boss or your colleagues.

Practical indications and tricks for correctly setting up a public speech

There are some fundamental rules to know and respect to ensure that what we say in front of an audience can be interesting, effective, ans above all persuasives.

To help you we will provide you with a complete list of little tricks and tips that will help you achieve a successful communication performance.

Setting up the speech

Preparation is essential therefore, especially if we are not used to speaking in public, we advise you to prepare the structure of your speech well in advance.

The suggestion is to analyze and explore the topics during preparation, making sure they are clear; only in this way will you be able to transmit them to your audience clearly and naturally. For an effective presentation, it is essential to plan the structure of your speech in advance, especially if you have no experience in public speaking. It is advisable to identify two or three key points and organize the performance around them. Let's also remember that people's attention span drops drastically after 10 minutes of listening; therefore, we try to concentrate the main message of the speech in the initial part of our speech.

During preparation, analyze and delve into the topics clearly to convey them naturally to the audience.

Preparation

Let's organize our speech in advance with a logical structure and repeat it out loud at least twice but avoid memorizing it word for word to avoid monotony and artificiality.

Breathing

To overcome anxiety, diaphragmatic breathing is helpful. Before going on stage, perform the exercise of inhaling through your nose, inflating your belly, and exhaling through your mouth, deflating your belly, with each phase lasting 5 seconds.

Mental predisposition

It's simply a matter of changing our mental approach: instead of focusing on negative expectations, let's focus on mentally preparing for success. Then visualize the audience applauding and anticipate the positive sensations you will feel before you even experience them.

Tone of voice and posture

Vary your tone of voice throughout your speech, pausing to emphasize important points and adjusting the intensity as needed. Control your facial expressions, hand gestures and posture to communicate effectively. Pronounce the words clearly and calmly, preferring quality in the transmission of concepts over quantity. Also avoid monotonous or excessively loud tones, looking for a variety that avoids both monotony and constant agitation.

Intonation and emphasis are truly essential elements in successful communication. If our tone is too low, monotonous or rushed, we could end up boring or distracting the audience. Adapt the tone to the situation: some parts require calm, others energy. Modulation is acquired with practice, involving the actors' approach a little in their interpretation. Practice paying attention to intonation by dedicating a few repetitions. Pronounce the words clearly, avoiding affectations and adapting to the content. Intentionally vary your tone, cadence, speed, and emphasis to avoid monotony while immersing yourself in the meaning of the speech. Focus only on the content, forgetting the audience, opinions and even yourself.

It is very important to have full control of our audience. This means that we will have to know not only the people we are referring to when we speak in public, but also the context in which it will happen. However, it is not always possible to gain insights into your audience. In this case you will need to do everything you can to get to know your listeners. A phase of studying the audience is necessary to be able to communicate with them effectively.

Always be careful when analyzing your audience

It is also essential to maintain complete control over our audience, understanding not only the people you will publicly address, but also the surrounding context. While obtaining detailed audience insights may not always be possible or at least easy, it is equally important to do everything you can to understand your listeners. Carrying out an in-depth study of the public is therefore decisive for effective communication with them.

The best way to attract attention and involve the public is to arouse an intense emotional state in people (we have already talked about this in previous chapters).

Use narration

To capture attention and engage your audience, it is effective to generate intense emotional reactions in people. Using narration, telling anecdotes, personal experiences or stories relevant to the topic, is the optimal method to stimulate interest, persuade and facilitate understanding.

The use of storytelling is one of the most used and efficient techniques in public communication. Storytelling, despite being a neutral technique, can be addressed to various purposes thanks to its universal nature:

✓ In a commercial context, it serves to persuade, sell and differentiate the narrator from the competition, highlighting personal and original elements.

✓ In politics, it is used to acquire new supporters and voters.

✓ In marketing, it aims to capture the audience's attention, stimulate needs and create a relationship based on trust.

✓ In advertising, it is used to promote the brand and increase the visibility of the company.

To ensure the effectiveness of storytelling, it is essential that the narrative follows a structure familiar to those who must deliver a persuasive and effective speech. Furthermore, it is essential to insert unique elements that can generate emotions. Narrating stories involves giving voice to a character that is engaging in the eyes of users. It is essential that the audience completely identify with the narrator, who does not have to be perfect, but credible. Every story told should convey a clear message, and to do so, the narrator must adopt an easily recognizable point of view. The objective of the message must be unambiguous and meaningful.

If you then have the opportunity to share personal experiences, you will be able to tangibly convey the impression of authenticity, reliability and authority to that specific audience. Real episodes are extraordinarily effective, because the truth makes the difference. If it is not possible to recount direct experiences, it is still essential to construct a plausible story.

Use quotation marks

To emphasize key moments and highlight significant messages, it can be advantageous to use quotation marks. To optimize their use, it is advisable to avoid excesses, use them in moderation and, above all, contextualize them in the context of the speech.

To effectively organize topics and consolidate key concepts in memory, a useful tool is represented by mind maps. These not only facilitate the connection between one topic and another, but will also allow you to give a certain organicity, coherence and to follow the logical thread of the discussion, without getting lost in embarrassing silences or showing little mastery of the concepts.

Maintain a certain consistency between verbal and body language

Maintaining consistency between verbal language and body language is essential. It is necessary to involve the whole person in verbal expression. Learning to manage body language goes beyond simple imitation of gestures and requires careful mastery of each movement. An open posture, relaxed shoulders and feet well anchored to the ground in balance, combined with a strong and confident tone of voice, conveys confidence both to the interlocutors and to us during communication. Personal safety translates into reliability, contributing to being listened to attentively. Body language is not limited to the hands; it involves the entire body and its way of communicating non-verbally to the audience.

The position of the feet when interacting with others is also significant. Belief in the conveyed message requires total body involvement in the speech. Body language constantly provides subtle signals to the audience about your inner state of mind. If you are nervous or don't believe in your speech, the audience will sense it. Consistency between verbal communication and body language is essential. Practice, especially through video recording, is the best method to improve and ensure effective and authentic communication.

Learn to work on your language, adapting it to your audience

Learn to modulate your language according to your audience, using words that are understandable to your listeners. In a medical conference, for example, it is common to use complex medical terms, as the audience expects specialized terminology. Fitting in this way not only demonstrates professionalism but also avoids looking inadequate.

On the other hand, if we are addressing a less expert audience, it is important to make the language more accessible, avoiding technicalities and using a suitable communicative tone. Adaptation of language is really essential to overcome barriers with the audience and maintain their attention, especially when the goal is to persuade the listener to take a specific action. Being convincing, confident and clear is crucial in this context.

Effectively manage a public speech

What's the best way to start a speech in front of an audience? Often, when writing a speech, there is a tendency to focus predominantly on the conclusion. However, it is essential to give equal, if not more, importance to the beginning of our speech.

The opening of your speech is of fundamental importance for several reasons:

✓ In some situations, the audience may not be familiar with us, and our first words will be our initial introduction.

✓ The initial moments will influence the degree of interest or hostility on the part of our audience.

✓ Openness determines the general atmosphere of our intervention.

✓ This is the time when we need to capture the public's attention.

✓ It helps to create empathy with those who listen to us.

Below are examples of the most common ways to start a speech.

Starting from humility

Start with humility, opting for the classic strategy of "excusatio propter infirmitatem", in which we apologize to the public for not being up to our role. However, we must avoid devaluing ourselves and instead underline the vastness and fascinating complexity of the topic, expressing the hope of being able to summarize it during the time available and inviting the public to evaluate the result.

Use humor

Also introduce your speech with humor, adopting the strategy of "excusatio propter infirmitatem" in the form of a self-deprecating joke. The audience appreciates the speaker's self-irony. You can very well take inspiration from the humorous and sarcastic phrases of famous people, such as:

"There are times when everything is fine: don't be scared, it doesn't last." -Jules Renard.

"The best things in life are immoral, illegal, or fattening." - George Bernard Shaw.

"Don't take life too seriously. You won't get out of this alive." - Elbert Hubbard.

Now it's time to state our thesis

After the "excusatio", if we choose this type of strategy, it is essential to explicitly mention the thesis we intend to prove. Begin the speech by clearly explaining the thesis you want to support. Before speaking, ask yourself two essential questions: What do I want to express? What is the thesis I am supporting? This clarity will make us aware of what is relevant to us. Take a piece of paper and list the essential concepts, not worrying about the number or sequence yet, but making sure they are relevant to the thesis and coherent.

And finally, the rhetorical question

We can begin our speech using one of the most recognizable rhetorical figures, the rhetorical question. This type of question doesn't actually require an answer, as the answer is often implicit in the question itself. To better understand how this works, consider a practical example: "Don't you think today is a bad day too?" The use of the rhetorical question is aimed at emphasizing an idea, both within a larger speech and in a shorter and more concise one. It is important to note that rhetorical questions differ from open-ended questions in that they are not asked to obtain an explicit answer.

To start a public speech in an impactful way, we can opt for a provocative or shocking statement, aimed at surprising the audience and capturing their attention.

In this eighth chapter we have shown concrete examples of persuasive communication, such as the interaction between boss and employees, accompanied by practical suggestions for communicating with staff on a daily basis. Advice was also provided on how to establish effective and persuasive communication with our superior, with indications on what to avoid saying and examples of conversations that can make a good impression. Plus, we've given you full access to all the best advice on how to communicate persuasively during a job interview, including practical examples. Finally, suggestions were offered on how to effectively address a public speech, underlining the importance of speaking correctly in public, and providing practical advice and concrete examples for successfully managing a public speech. Having concluded the fourth part, in the next part we will discuss all the persuasive communication techniques applied for the purpose of sales.

PART FIVE: PERSUASION APPLIED TO SALES

In this fifth part of the book on effective communication, we will talk about how to apply persuasion techniques directly to sales. The first part will therefore cover all the strategies to be implemented to achieve all our sales objectives, while the second will focus on managing all the objections during persuasive selling. By removing these obstacles, you can achieve any sales goal and succeed in business.

Chapter 9: The best persuasive sales strategies

In this ninth chapter, we will show all the best persuasive sales techniques. This set of techniques and strategies, in fact, will be very useful to you on a professional level. In fact, strategies will be shown to capture the attention of our interlocutor when we express an idea, to convince him to purchase our product or service and to close sales negotiations. This part is therefore dedicated to anyone with a business growth objective because, let's be clear, without sales a company has no future. For this reason, it is essential to have at least one competent figure in your team, capable of communicating effectively to increase sales. It could also be you: you already have the tools to capture and maintain customer attention. Here we will explain how to leverage his concerns, thus positioning the purchase of the product as the ideal solution to resolve them, without however falling into excessive intrusiveness which could only be counterproductive. As we will explain better in this chapter, to be able to make the most of persuasion skills it is above all necessary to try to solve the customer's problems, and to present oneself as the best solution. Therefore, it is not only necessary to know the reasons why each of our potential customers should buy the product, but also those that can be solved by purchasing the product.

A step-by-step guide: how to best close our deals

As mentioned above, there are sales strategies that will allow us to make the most of the effective and persuasive communication that we have learned so far. Let's see in more detail what the best applicable persuasive selling strategies are.

The first step is to get to know our audience as best as possible

When it comes to convincing someone to buy anything, the first thing we need to do is know who we're talking to. It's about being perfectly aware of who our potential customers are, what their way of communicating is; in addition to all this, we should also be aware of what their interests and problems are. This last point will better allow us to create more suitable content and messages to attract their attention.

In fact, it will be the creation of the most suitable content of our message that will determine the success of the communicative relationship between us and whoever is on the other side. Our potential customers will be interested in what we have to say when they feel called into question, when they have the perception that the message is aimed specifically at them and that they will only be able to benefit from it.

Now is the time to make a value proposition

As we have often repeated in this book, communication and persuasion are very different concepts and distant from manipulation. This differentiation is due to the value proposition.

It is therefore a question of the fact that the persuasive one is a value proposition, or rather a short positioning statement, which is very important to make our interlocutors understand why our product or service could be useful for them. To succeed in the aim of formulating a proposal of correct value, you must be able to answer, as a first step, the following questions:

✓ How important is my product?

✓ What problems or needs does it solve?

✓ Why would I be tempted to buy it?

✓ What are its strong points and what makes it different from all the others?

✓ What are its weaknesses?

✓ What are the consumer's questions or concerns?

By asking these questions, you can get a clear idea of how much your product or service is worth and how it can help people solve their problems.

Now, the questions that every potential customer will ask themselves will be:

✓ Is what they're saying really interesting to me?

✓ What will I really get by purchasing this product or service?

Putting ourselves on the customer's side, the objective is therefore to know how to answer all these questions. To give a practical example, instead of starting the conversation by talking about us or our product, the conversation could simply be about what we can concretely do for our interlocutor. In other words, a proposal will be made that already has the value of a possible resolution of various problems for our potential customers.

Now we listen to our customers and invite them to ask questions

Listening carefully to our potential customer allows us to understand what their resistance, doubts or desires are. This is truly valuable information, which will be useful for us to direct the conversation in a way that conveys greater trust to our potential customer or get them to ask as many questions as possible.

Every time the customer becomes interested in us, it gives us the full opportunity to create and convey our persuasive message.

The other key elements that we must then take into consideration are:

✓ The audience to which our product or service is aimed.

✓ The description of what we want to sell.

✓ The advantage it offers to potential customers.

✓ Tangible evidence, such as a statistic or a personal result that we have already obtained thanks to the sale of that specific product or service.

Keeping these elements in mind helps us not only to understand our product or service very well, but also to involve our audience more in the sale.

Now persuasion comes into play

We remind you that "convincing" does not just refer to the art of persuading our customers. If we are not the first to be 100% sure of what we are saying, we certainly will not be able to convince others. We are often our own greatest saboteurs since we have the absurd claim of convincing others of something but, being unconvinced ourselves to begin with, what emerges from our speech is the exact opposite. Did you remember that at the beginning of this guide we also mentioned non-verbal language? If our actions do not practically reflect our words, giving little confidence and cause to our vocal expression, it will be difficult to obtain any credibility. The alignment between body language and speech is essential avoiding doubts in our interlocutors. Demonstrating competence, experience and reliability is also essential to instilling confidence and achieving positive results in situations like those you have faced. An authority figure who demonstrates ability is more persuasive and receives greater acceptance. To positively influence others, it is also relevant to be able to embody authority by demonstrating clarity, confidence and confidence in one's abilities, especially in dealing with needs and problems. Persuasion requires a confident attitude, with confidence in our ability to help others, combined with a mastery of discourse. This approach will capture the customer's attention, pushing them to take the necessary actions to close a sale.

Motivate to action

To push someone to perform an action, it is effective to show it through your gaze, body movements or by performing it yourself, as in using your product.

The gaze represents a very powerful tool in persuasive communication, since it is a technique to induce the user to concentrate his attention in the direction indicated by the gaze. So, let's not limit ourselves to simply selecting the most suitable words, but let's emphasize our message with looks and gestures that highlight our message even more. By associating words with body movements, we have the concrete possibility that the interlocutor can remember them vividly, making the concept more tangible and memorable. This approach is fundamental to prevent words from remaining abstract and being forgotten. To leave a lasting impression, we invite the potential customer to personally experience what we just said in our speech.

We use logic and emotions

To start a deal effectively, we start by focusing on the benefits for customers. Subsequently, it is appropriate to highlight the real characteristics of the product on sale.

It is also advisable to consolidate our credibility by presenting specific product data or our professional qualifications. It is therefore a matter of citing authoritative sources, mentioning experiences with other clients or presenting case studies are also effective strategies.

This type of strategy aims, in fact, to influence the logic of our interlocutor. At the beginning of a negotiation, emotions and instinct push the potential customer towards an offer; Next, they look for rational reasons to justify the purchase decision. A direct and effective method to engage logic is to use "why." Instead of making simple claims, we always show the benefits and objectives that our offer can guarantee. We encourage and guide the potential customer in a reasoning that will convince him or her that our proposal is the right choice for him or her.

We stimulate the imagination of the potential customer

Engaging the imagination of our potential customers is an effective means of arousing emotions and satisfying their desires. Sales focuses, in a practical and direct way, on understanding and satisfying people's desires. To make our communication more persuasive and our offer more convincing, we allow the interlocutor to enrich our words with their own imagination. Allowing them to clearly visualize what they will achieve increases desire and need. Imagination, connected to the world of dreams, is a powerful element, especially when communicating without visual support. Words and persuasive communication thus become fundamental to freeing the imagination during the conversation.

We limit the options to avoid indecision on the part of our interlocutor

Through persuasive communication, we can concretely convince our potential customer to adopt a specific idea or take a certain action. However, it is crucial at this point to avoid offering too many alternatives, as this could lead to decision paralysis. If the other person has many options in front of him, he may go a long time without making any decisions. To prevent this, after having outlined the desired outcome, we can provide some ways to achieve this outcome, thus ensuring that we push the other person to make a definitive choice. To guide the customer in the desired direction, the ideal approach usually involves offering 3 options. However, the recommended management consists in presenting one that is clearly not advantageous and to be excluded, thus leaving the actual choice between the remaining 2. Our role will then be to facilitate the purchasing decision for the potential customer, not by imposing it, but by assisting him in narrowing down the choice of the product we want him to purchase.

This also concludes our ninth chapter. To have a complete picture of persuasive communication with the aim of selling, in the next chapter we will take care of dismantling all objections and removing obstacles from our path.

Chapter 10: How to handle various objections and remove obstacles in persuasive selling

This tenth chapter will be very useful to you in order to remove any obstacle to your effective and persuasive communication. In fact, by being able to manage the various objections, you will be well prepared in the face of any unexpected event, ready to proceed towards our sales objectives. Let's see in detail how to manage all the objections of our potential customers.

How to handle all objections from our potential customers

Let's start directly with a list of all the effective strategies and techniques to be able to address and manage any potential objections from our interlocutor and to ensure that our communication can really hit the mark.

Build trust, always

In this case, empathy always comes into play, which will act as a catalyst to start real communication based on a relationship of mutual trust. Trust serves, precisely, to create that ideal climate to ensure that there are no objections. If we are able to get to know our potential customer in depth and understand it, on the other hand we will have the concrete possibility of analyzing their situation more broadly. This allows us to see any type of objection that might creep between us and them. Trust also serves us to ensure that our potential customer can express himself about it. The doubts that hold our customer back could concern his family situation, the opinions of others on his purchase or what the comments would be, for example from his wife or parents. children. Empathy, in this case, helps us go deeper and understand what is beyond the facade, and also be able to give confidence to our interlocutor by using the right words. Furthermore, we will be able to show understanding, and this will allow us to create a deeper relationship of trust and make them more likely to purchase our product or service.

To avoid objections we will always have to take into account what our customers really need

Understanding needs, as we have already said several times in this guide, is necessary to direct our message in the best way. If we cannot understand our potential customer's attitude or do not understand what is holding them back from purchasing, we can always ask them openly and bluntly.

In this case, we can always ask questions, about the doubts that keep our potential customers from deciding to buy and find ways to comfort and reassure them.

Never be afraid to be direct, but always try to maintain discretion and respect. Also carefully evaluate the context and act, accordingly, making your potential customer feel appreciated. Our offer should naturally resolve itself as the ideal solution for his needs, anticipating doubts and objectives. It is essential to identify the advantages so that the potential customer sees our offer as the preferred option to satisfy his desires. Once we have passed this step, we should then persuade him that making the purchase is the most advantageous and convenient choice for him or for her.

The "why not?" strategy

This is an approach that, according to a study by Dr. Stiff, significantly increases the chances of obtaining a favorable consensus after a firm refusal. This is because the other party often has difficulty coming up with objections that are robust enough to justify their initial response. When objections are weak, cognitive dissonance is created which pushes the interlocutor to reconsider their position to maintain coherence and reasonableness.

Now we use the most effective and persuasive phrases that will increase our sales

Winning statements to successfully promote our product is a strategic element for businesses and online sellers of all sizes. A single phrase strategically placed, such as at the beginning of a digital catalog or as a call to action in an article, has the potential to capture users' attention and convert a simple visitor into a customer. In this case, it involves studying and repeating the most incisive and persuasive phrases capable of boosting our sales.

The origin of our products is certified

Using phrases such as, "Our product is completely made in... to our standards". Using the "Made in" label offers the possibility of formulating various phrases that facilitate the sale of products and services. However, it is also advisable to avoid deception: If customers detect that we are presenting our business or products untruthfully, it could lead to serious purchase issues. People appreciate quality, but they do not tolerate lies. Therefore, we only use this statement if it is actually accurate for our situation.

Make it clear that the product or service is absolutely essential

An effective phrase, which could really turn the sale around, obviously aimed at our potential customer, could be once you experience our product or service, it will become indispensable for you! Or: its quality will win you over." "By trying it, your day will be transformed for the better!" "By giving it as a gift, you will receive eternal gratitude." The possibilities for creating engaging sentences are endless. The basic approach is to present the reader with a promise of happiness, improvement of daily life or tangible benefit. Furthermore, we really have the freedom and possibility to personalize the message according to our needs and the audience we have in front of us.

Up-to-date, fast, intuitive: just as our customer prefers

If our customers do not express such a wish, we will do it for them. Then concisely summarize the benefits of your product or service and suggest that these features might be appealing to the listener. In less than a minute, you'll have a catchy phrase that instantly explains why someone might want your product or service.

Money Back Guarantee

At this point, we ask you if you have ever considered the option of guaranteeing the complete satisfaction of your customers with a refund policy? This practice is now widespread, especially in the e-commerce sector. Offering the option to return a product within a specified period and get a refund without penalty can significantly reassure customers. However, carefully evaluate the feasibility of such a guarantee, as it could increase sales in a short time.

Small discounts

We are all always looking for savings and, in this case, the promises of discounts irresistibly attract our eyes. This is why we can opt for the classic phrase "save up to....", followed by a percentage of our choice, as a sure strategy to increase sales, especially among those who constantly seek the opportunity for maximum convenience in purchases.

Also include service and maintenance

One of the main concerns that affects potential customers every day and that often holds them back from completing a particular purchase concerns post-purchase assistance. Ensuring immediate support without additional costs in the event of a defective product is in the best interest of the customer. But if you want to offer support or maintenance as part of the offer, make sure you specify this clearly not only in the terms and conditions, but also prominently to encourage purchase.

Create a short-term deadline

How many times have you read sentences that indicate a deadline? "You can purchase at no additional cost within two days" or "Offer valid for the next 48 hours, hurry!". Communicating a time limit strikes a particularly sensitive chord with consumers. No one wants to miss the opportunity to purchase a product or service at a discounted price. This is undoubtedly one of the most commonly used success phrases and will allow you to close your deals.

Offer full availability for a quote or consultancy

A simple and warm invitation to receive a quote or advice is a recommended approach towards an undecided customer. Sometimes, companies stay away from the sales process, but it is essential to demonstrate maximum availability before, during and after the purchase. This phrase communicates to the customer that we are at their disposal for every need and will create a relationship of greater trust.

This indicated above was the last effective strategy to overcome any objection from any potential customer faced with one of our products and services. In this fifth part, in fact, we have addressed a specific aspect of persuasive communication: effective sales strategies. Gaining proficiency in these strategies will be extremely beneficial in the professional context, allowing us to gain the attention of the interlocutor when presenting an idea, persuade customers about our product or service and successfully close sales negotiations. So, if you are a sales professional and want to increase your results, spend more time perfecting these strategies.

PART SIX: NON-VERBAL COMMUNICATION

After talking about sales and persuasive communication, all the techniques and objections to be removed, in this sixth part we will deal with a topic of equal importance: non-verbal communication. We have dedicated a specific section of this guide precisely because of the importance of body language in giving coherence to what we are communicating. In fact, we will talk about all the aspects that involve non-verbal language and how to correctly manage our body language.

Chapter 11: Body language and non-verbal communication

In this eleventh chapter, non-verbal communication will be described in detail, what advantages it brings and what communication skills it allows us to develop more. Finally, there will be a complete description of the importance of non-verbal language and how it can help us make our communication even more effective and persuasive.

A small description of non-verbal language

We reveal one of the key secrets for persuasive and effective communication: in addition to using the appropriate verbal language, knowing how to correctly use body language and non-verbal messages gives that aura of coherence that makes our message strong and above all authoritative. The definition of Body language refers to nonverbal signals that we sometimes use unconsciously to communicate and includes all nonverbal communication. Unlike verbal language, in fact, body language, not being guided by will, does not allow for ambiguity. If we think about it carefully, gestures, the way we move or look are very often in symbiosis or the opposite of verbal language, because unconsciously they can support it, reduce it or even contradict it. The non-verbal signals that make up the body language of a person are often able, precisely, to communicate much more than words. Body signals can include facial expressions, hand gestures, tone of voice and other body gestures. Moving the body in specific directions and making gestures is not just a superficial habit or a series of meaningless movements but plays a real role essential in the processing of verbal meanings in the brain. Experts say that body language represents a significant component of everyday communication, being able to convey much more about our thoughts or feelings than the words used.

Each of our non-verbal gestures transmits powerful messages, having the ability to establish a comfortable climate, generate trust and attract others, or to confuse and compromise the message we are trying to communicate. Even when we are silent, in fact, our non-verbal communication is active, and its various aspects can even contrast our words.

Understanding the true meaning of nonverbal behavior

Non-verbal behavior constitutes an essential element of our communication: we certainly can't ignore this! Truly effective communication takes advantage of the multiple information provided by facial expressions, tone of voice and gestures. To fully understand the role of the nonverbal, it is really important to recognize that it often conveys ambiguous messages. Trying to find definitive explanations for gestures such as crossing the arms, or the direction of the gaze is a strategy doomed to failure. Not only would we not get clear answers, but we could also complicate the situation. In fact, if we dedicate excessive attention to these signals and start to interpret them, we will lose our presence in the conversation, generating two unwanted effects:

1. We will miss crucial information because our focus will be on ourselves rather than others.

2. We will compromise the quality of communication, since we will be perceived as distracted (or hostile), reducing the interlocutor's motivation to speak.

Several studies highlight our limited ability to recognize lies, suggesting we should be cautious in our interpretations. If we wish to use body language to enhance our persuasive abilities, it is useful to know that this area is divided into four macro areas:

1. Illustrator gestures: They describe concepts through images, as in mime or silent cinema, where gestures replace verbal language.

2. Deictic movements: They accompany the words (I, you, this) and serve to concretely indicate something, either voluntarily or involuntarily, to strengthen the dialogue.

3. Revealing gestures: Involve involuntary actions, such as verbal slips, often linked to the culture or environment one belongs to.

4. Analogical gestures: They constitute totally involuntary forms of expression that originate from the unconscious, revealing our deepest thoughts and emotions in an almost completely truthful way.

The importance of non-verbal communication

We conclude this short chapter with the importance of verbal communication and the relative advantages it brings. Let's examine the benefits of a correct interpretation of the body and its language:

Develop our emotional awareness

Knowing how to read the body's signals allows us to better interpret the emotions and moods of other people. This also allows us to understand what they are really thinking or feeling. In this way, we will simply have the opportunity to respond in the most appropriate way, making our responses more appropriate and timelier. The ability to interpret body signals therefore favors a more accurate understanding of the emotions and moods of others, allowing us to discern what they really think or feel.

Facilitates building trust

Understanding nonverbal language allows us to use it strategically to build trust. We can consciously adopt nonverbal signals that indicate openness and sincerity, while also avoiding those that unintentionally convey lies, insecurity or secrets.

Express yourself clearly

Expressing your perspective clearly is an added benefit of understanding body language. We can deliberately integrate gestures and other nonverbal cues that support rather than oppose our point of view, communicating effectively and persuasively.

Give a positive impression of us

The conscious use of different elements of non-verbal communication helps to project confidence, emphasize our message and inspire trust, overall contributing to creating a good first impression.

A significant contribution in the workplace

Body language also plays a key role in sales strategies. When a seller adopts appropriate non-verbal communication, he can create an equally spontaneous, positive and involuntary impression on the buyer. It is equally essential to observe the prospect's body language to evaluate the effectiveness of our interaction.

Customer trust is manifested through:

✓ Willingly maintaining eye contact
✓ Positioning yourself frontally, showing the front part of the torso
✓ Nodding your head compulsively during a conversation.

Having examined its importance and benefits, in the next chapter, we will show you how to understand and manage body language correctly.

Chapter 12: Learning to understand and use body language

Non-verbal communication, as we have seen, is made up of all those nuances that go beyond the simple words we pronounce. It is made of gestures, poses that can make our communication stronger or, on the contrary, make it inconsistent and make us less credible. In this twelfth chapter, in fact, we will help you understand how to make good use of our body language to ensure that our communication acquires greater authority, coherence and is completely unassailable.

We understand body language

Body language is not something made up in the air, based on uncertain ideas and unfounded hypotheses. We know, in fact, that the study of body language is the result of a long process of scientific studies and tests conducted both in the laboratory and in the daily lives of each of us. Therefore, it is not something that has stopped at simple theory. And just as the study of body language is not just a set of conjectures but a process of practices and experience (on its understanding and correct use), it is necessary to practice a lot to understand its true meaning and use it to make our communication even clearer, and powerful. Body language, in other words, is about practice. For us, the easiest way to understand how nonverbal language works is to start practicing it, first of all, with our family and closest social circles. This is because, by having in-depth knowledge, we will not only be able to understand other people's non-verbal language more easily, guess what they are thinking or if they are really listening to you, but also to use gestures, postures or expressions that allow us to best convey what we communicate. And do it in all honesty. By being frank and sincere, it will also be possible for us to obtain feedback on our ability to read or use our body. To best learn this art, we can start by observing everyone around us. Practice will help us not only to perfectly learn the art of body language but also to use the conscious part of our brain to the detriment of the unconscious one, to observe more deeply rather than repeat the gestures of others. When we have perfectly learned to manage body language and by observing others with a detached spirit, we will have the concrete possibility of making fewer errors of evaluation, since above all we will be able to analyze the situations that happen to us using only the rational part of the mind.

Complete guide to understand the meaning of body movements

Understanding body language is something global, that is not limited only to the movement of the eyes, or mouth, or facial expressions. Learning to read body language is not limited to one or two parts of the body, but involves everything, absolutely everything! Let's see together all the areas of the body involved in non-verbal communication.

Facial expressions

Let's start with facial expressions, the very ones that we cannot control because they are often unconscious. Our facial expressions, in fact, can reveal what we really think. This is why you really need to pay a lot of attention to your face. Body language is extremely expressive and is above all a source of information on an emotional level without the need to say a word. Furthermore, facial expressions are universal. How many times have you heard the expression: if I don't say it, my face says it for me! Expressions, therefore, can show a range of emotions.

Among the emotions that we can express thanks to our face are:

- ✓ Contempt
- ✓ Happiness
- ✓ Fear
- ✓ Anger
- ✓ Shame
- ✓ Sadness

But how do we actually express emotions thanks to our facial expressions? A study on facial expressions and body language showed that raising eyebrows and smiling are the most reliable facial expressions, as they convey both friendliness and confidence. Touching your eyebrows and scratching them, however, in body language is the typical gesture of those who want to hide their skepticism in a context in which it would be inappropriate. Specifically, let's see how our facial expressions reflect the emotions mentioned above.

- ✓ Happiness: Wide smile, bright eyes.
- ✓ Sadness: Furrowed forehead, lowered lips.
- ✓ Anger: Fixed gaze, furrowed eyebrows.
- ✓ Surprise: Eyes wide open, mouth open.
- ✓ Disgust: Scrunched nose, tight lips.
- ✓ Fear: Eyebrows raised, eyes wide.
- ✓ Amazement: Interested look, slight smile.
- ✓ Confusion: Frowned eyebrows, puzzled expression.

The eyes

Eyes play a key role in face-to-face communication and allow us to understand a lot about our interlocutor.

- ✓ Eye contact, when kept moderate, denotes interest; however, if prolonged, it can appear threatening.

- ✓ Avoidant glances or lowered gaze may indicate anxiety, embarrassment, or a desire to hide something.
- ✓ In body language, looking away or lowering your eyes during uncomfortable questions can suggest a gap between the words spoken and the perceived truth.
- ✓ Widely dilated pupils may suggest excitement, attraction, or desire, while constricted, smaller pupils might indicate anger or a negative mood.
- ✓ Rolling your eyes in body language can express frustration or resignation.
- ✓ Frequent blinking may indicate discomfort, while poor blinking may reveal intentional control of eye movements.
- ✓ Widening your eyes is a sign of interest and sympathy.

Mouth

The mouth is responsible for significant signals in body language. Let's see which ones:
- ✓ Smiling can express happiness, approval, sarcasm or cynicism.
- ✓ A tight-lipped smile often indicates discomfort, but the person still tries to appear friendly and courteous.
- ✓ Biting your lower lip can signal insecurity or worry.
- ✓ Covering your mouth to hide a reaction, such as a sincere smile or smirk, can be polite if you're yawning or coughing, but it can also indicate an attempt to hide disapproval.

Arm

A person's arms are involved in nonverbal communication, with examples of body language including:
- ✓ Keep your arms close to your body to attract less attention.
- ✓ Expand your arms to project authority, grandeur, or menace.
- ✓ Crossing your arms and keeping them folded indicates feelings of self-protection, defense, or closure.
- ✓ Touching your arm can indicate a sign of intimacy.
- ✓ In nonverbal communication, hugging can express love, passion, or even hate, representing a wide range of emotions.

Feet and legs

Feet and legs, although not the first body parts considered in nonverbal communication, play a rather important role in the psychology of body language such as:
- ✓ Both feet pointing towards us and in a V shape indicates interest.
- ✓ Both feet pointed away from us may suggest disinterest.
- ✓ Crossed legs may indicate that the person feels distant or uninterested.
- ✓ In body language, crossing your legs can express a desire for self-protection.

Posture

The position of the trunk and posture are fundamental elements for interpreting body language and non-verbal communication. Posture can convey different information about a person's emotional state and suggest personality characteristics, such as confidence, openness or submission. Sitting upright can suggest concentration and attention, while leaning the body forward can be interpreted as a sign of boredom or indifference. Furthermore, turning your back while speaking openly communicates disinterest or aggression.

The jaw

The jaw clearly reflects the mood of our interlocutor. For example, a clenched jaw indicates stress and discomfort. However, this behavior may not be an immediate response to the current situation but may arise from an unconscious thought not related to the present moment. Therefore, when we notice a clenched jaw, it could indicate that our interlocutor is perhaps pretending to listen to us, while in reality he is reflecting on something that worries him, thus manifesting the stress associated with that thought.

To nod

Nodding (or nodding) is a common involuntary behavior during conversations, often indicative of agreement with the speaker. This gesture is widely used in sales, as it establishes a favorable bond between the seller and the customer. While salespeople may nod to create connections, they can sometimes do so even when they disagree internally. There are three variations of this gesture. Let's see them together:

✓ Tilting your head slowly: in many circumstances, this gesture indicates the interlocutor's attention to what we are saying, but sometimes it can just be a way of feigning interest. Here, the focus is less on the content heard and more on the involuntary act of nodding, used deliberately to simulate involvement.

✓ Nodding at a moderate speed: whoever performs this gesture is sincerely agreeing with their interlocutor. His interest is so high that his head movement is semi-voluntary, with an initial involuntary thrust deliberately accentuated to emphasize enthusiasm.

✓ Nodding rapidly: This type of nodding often indicates anxiety and a strong desire for approval. When someone shakes their head convulsively during an interaction, they may be concerned about your opinion of them.

The palms of the hands

Hand positions also offer valuable information on attitudes, both of our interlocutors and our own. For example, if we show our palms facing upwards, we are communicating trust, sincerity and honesty to our interlocutor. This gesture is often used involuntarily to reinforce the meaning of our words. Conversely, when we keep our palms facing down or resting on the table, we are projecting authority, power and strength in communication.

Proxemics

Proxemics, a branch of semiology, examines gestures, behaviors, spaces and distances in the context of communication between two or more people, both verbal and non-verbal. This concept, introduced by anthropologist Edward Twitchell Hall, specifically concerns the distance maintained during interactions between individuals.

Thanks to proxemics, it is possible to evaluate from afar the dynamics and freedom of movement between two people in conversation. The ideal is when you interact standing up, possibly facing each other.

Hall, in his study, outlined four levels of social distancing in different situations:

✓ Intimate distance (15-45 cm): indicates a relationship of great comfort with often physical involvement.

✓ Personal distance (45-120 cm): observed between family members or close friends. Freedom of movement during the conversation reflects the degree of intimacy.

✓ Social distance (120-360 cm): represents the distance in a conversation between acquaintances with good relationships, but without deep knowledge. The degree of knowledge is reflected in the distance between the interlocutors.

✓ Audience distance (over 360 cm): this is the distance adopted during public speeches or conversations between two unknown people, such as in a job interview.

Having finished the discussion on proxemics, we have seen in this chapter and in the fifth part that a determining element in persuasive communication is precisely non-verbal language. The key to effective and persuasive communication lies, in fact, in the ability to adequately use body language and non-verbal signals. Gestures, movement and gaze often follow a path parallel to verbal language, being able to unconsciously support, attenuate or contradict it. We have understood how to interpret non-verbal language and decipher implicit messages through the gestures of our interlocutor.

We also explained the full importance of understanding these signals to guide the conversation towards our desired goal. Furthermore, we examined another dimension of nonverbal language: proxemics. This discipline, related to semiology, analyzes gestures, behaviors, spaces and distances in communication between two or more people, both verbal and non-verbal, representing one of the subcategories in the study of non-verbal communication. As for communication in general, we have finished our main speech.

In the last chapter of this guide, which will be a bonus, we will deal with a very important aspect that should never be overlooked when it comes to communicating effectively and persuasively: our image, but above all the perception and value we attribute to ourselves. Self-esteem, as we will see, is essential to making ourselves perceived not only as people of value, but also to give that aura of certainty and validity to what we are communicating.

Bonus Chapter: Importance of image and self-esteem

Before leaving with this guide, we wanted to dedicate an entire chapter to a fundamental aspect that distinguishes us from being successful communicators or not, namely self-esteem and the image we project externally. In fact, if we want to learn persuasive communication in depth, to be fully capable of impressing and changing the ideas and opinions of others, knowing only the basic principles or techniques of persuasion is not entirely sufficient. As we have seen, in the course of this practical guide, some of the techniques to be more persuasive communicators or to become more convincing towards those in front of us are quite simple, others imply a certain degree of experience which is obtained with continuous and constant practice, but also thanks to a good dose of self-esteem and confidence in one's abilities. There are therefore some basic elements that are essential to completely mastering the art of persuasive communication. As we will explain below, these basic elements are represented by self-esteem and the importance we give to ourselves and our image.

Self-esteem: why is it fundamental?

Having full self-confidence and high self-esteem, let's start by saying, is not a prerogative of many people. Indeed: since it is not an innate ability but one that we develop through experiences and various positive or negative factors, many of us do not have a natural inclination to have a great perception of ourselves. In fact, there are people who show strong confidence and great self-esteem, while others are shyer and more closed in their own world and show their insecurity at first glance. Now think about when you will have to communicate. We have already said it several times, a closed attitude certainly does not help, while a safer, more open one gives others the security necessary to be "persuaded". Being persuasive therefore requires a good dose of self-confidence because the impression we must give, if we want others to follow us or listen to us and above all demonstrate confidence in what we do or say, is that we ourselves are the ones who are absolutely sure of what we are doing or communicating. If, for example, we are unsure about a topic, our knowledge or how others perceive us, we should be able to prove it. Or being so good that not even a minimum of insecurity is visible to others. Success in the field of persuasion is achieved only if we therefore demonstrate that we have a strong and decisive personality or if we are people who do not know what insecurity is. Low self-esteem, in fact, negatively affects work, study, emotional relationships and the relationship with oneself, limiting our action and choices. For this reason, if you are not a great admirer of your person, you will need to seriously work on it to be successful not only in the field of communication, but in any field. Changing your self-perception and consequently increasing your self-esteem is not always a simple task: there are exercises and a lot of practice and self-awareness to do, but it is important to understand that it is something changeable, which can therefore change and certainly improve. In this part we want to give you the right indications to gain greater self-confidence. Below you will find some useful tips to have more confidence and perceive yourself as a person of value.

We always start with our strengths

One of the essential first steps in the process of building self-esteem is the full recognition of one's potential, our strengths and our qualities. Be careful, this is something that is really easier said than done. Those with low self-esteem, in fact, tend not to be aware of their resources rather than recognize them. Furthermore, those who blame themselves easily and often are more lenient in judging others than in judging themselves.

Now, the most functional way to develop self-esteem in this sense is to use a daily diary in which we write down 3 things we liked about ourselves during the day and then re-read the list the next morning. We could also write down our strengths and re-read the list in the evening before going to sleep. This always helps us understand how much we are worth.

Always achieve feasible mini-goals

How many times have we set ourselves big goals complete with unrealistic and unattainable ambitions? And every time we failed to meet these expectations; our self-esteem plummeted. Now, the best thing is to rethink our objectives in terms of feasibility, perhaps downsizing them or looking for the possibility of concretely achieving them. Goals work, in fact, only if they help trigger a virtuous circle, in which every goal we achieve is followed by a reward that subsequently motivates us to achieve even more important goals. It must be, in practice, a step-by-step process. Also think about the fact that breaking down macro-objectives into many small goals to achieve may not only be simpler but is a fundamental job for acquiring a positive self-image and increasing self-esteem. Every time the mini goal is reached, we feel stronger, more aware and ready to continue successfully.

Avoid making excuses

Blaming yourself and feeling sorry for yourself are attitudes that should absolutely be avoided when it comes to building your own, because they are two sabotaging enemies. Often, in fact, we look for excuses or blame to solve our problems. Or we continue to dredge up the past with lots of regret and victimization. Now, what we really need to understand is that we cannot change the past, but we can intervene in the present and the future. It is simply about taking full responsibility that only we are able to manage our emotions and what happens in our lives. Taking responsibility, therefore, means investigating what we are doing in life that not only is not working but prevents you from obtaining the desired results. The next step is to focus our attention on the solutions instead of the problem. About the present instead of the past.

Let's change our habits even in small steps

Even our habits are often unhealthy and do not allow us to evolve. Think about it, how many bad habits do we have, and would we like to change them? Let's start with everyday life. Choose a small habit that you want to eliminate or change for the better. Dedicate the next 30 days to it and then move on to the next habit.

Overcome the fear of failure

You have no idea how paralyzing our fears of failure are in allowing us to succeed. In fact, fear often pushes us to avoid situations and people that could actually only be beneficial, which only further reinforces low self-esteem and prevents us from growing. The important thing to do is that, when things go wrong, and unfortunately this really happens to everyone, it is important to change the way we evaluate what happened. Changing perspective, in this case, means that we must always consider that failure, however frustrating and painful it is, has a truly essential function, because only by trial and error can the process of self-improvement be activated. There are no people who have not gone through failure and become successful. Simply, when everything seems to be going wrong, they have developed less destructive and more functional thoughts and from the relapse they have pushed themselves to improve.

Take concrete action

How could we ever have a better perception of ourselves if we don't actually do something to improve? What if, in fact, we don't practice being better people? This does not mean obsessively chasing perfection, it does not exist and believing that we can achieve it is always something very dangerous. We need to find something that really interests us and makes us passionate, but they must be interests and passions that fuel our personalities, and at the same time allow us to take care of relationships and our physical appearance. This allows us to project a better image of ourselves in our minds. Being passionate people, full of interests not only improves our image through the mirror of others but will also make us self-reflect as better people.

Always keep your promises

We keep the promises we make, not only towards others, but also towards ourselves: every time we fail to keep a promise, we lose confidence in ourselves. In fact, if we want to acquire greater self-esteem, let's make some promises ourselves, make them realistic and above all let's keep them. This pushes us more and more to improve.

Sport as a regular habit

A healthy habit is to train regularly, an activity that will help you regain confidence in yourself.

Maintaining a regular exercise practice goes beyond improving health, well-being and fitness; represents a fundamental learning experiences for life. Every physical activity requires resilience, determination and motivation, helping to strengthen not only the muscles but also the spirit.

Remember to smile

Facing problems with a smile allows us to improve our days; if we can't solve our problem, facing it with the right amount of irony allows us to let go of our worries and lighten up. Let us therefore never forget to smile; it's a simple, almost obvious but powerful gesture to improve mood and increase self-esteem, even if sometimes it's not simple.

Think more about solutions

Focusing on solutions is more constructive than constantly telling yourself how difficult life seems. Let us therefore avoid obsessive thoughts about problems and learn to direct our attention towards possible solutions.

Altruism as an ingredient for improvement

Contrary to what one might think, those who show more anxiety and insecurity are often centered on themselves, while those who enjoy serenity and security dedicate themselves to others. Instead of constantly focusing on us, let's try to sincerely dedicate time to helping others, listening to them and offering support.

Stop procrastinating! To free ourselves from procrastination and improve our well-being, we choose to carry forward something every day that we have been putting off for too long. Postponing makes no sense and above all it keeps us away from our main goals, making us increasingly insecure and disheartened.

The fundamental importance of learning to say no

It's about clearly defining the boundaries with the outside world, opening the doors to those who can enter with respect and closing them when necessary. Select the people around you carefully, preferring those who recognize our value. The careful choice of companies is therefore crucial since bad social circles can really influence our lives in a positive or negative way.

It is therefore a question of connecting deeply with our values and needs, acting in harmony with them. Ignoring our inner voice increases the risk of conforming to the expectations of others.

Learning to say no is essential to pursuing and achieving our goals. There is no escape; establishing priorities is always the best step to avoid being overwhelmed by commitments and duties.

Knowing how to say yes when necessary

In this case, it's about becoming fully aware of what we love and what arouses our enthusiasm and running towards it. Setting aside time for passions is key to preventing frustration and tiredness. Let us therefore face our fears and always try to be open to new experiences: only in this way can we say yes to what good can come into our lives. Avoiding what scares us, in fact, could lead us to build an insidious prison around us, limiting ourselves in fear.

Celebrate achievements

Celebrating our accomplishments is a great way to not only boost our self-esteem but also realize our goals through small, planned steps. It is therefore about recognizing the progress we have made and rewarding ourselves for what we have achieved. We often neglect to appreciate small successes, but doing so will help strengthen our sense of self-efficacy and gather energy. This attitude will help us overcome obstacles without giving up at the first setback.

These that we have provided above are just practical suggestions for boosting self-esteem, but the path is gradual and complex, with daily challenges. Overcoming obstacles with commitment leads to a positive change in self-esteem and greater self-confidence. And it is something we must do every day, especially if we want to improve in the field of persuasive and effective communication.

The importance of our image in persuasive communication

The relevance of the image we have of ourselves within communicative persuasion lies in its influence on the success of social relationships. Every day, during our meetings, we try to present a positive image of ourselves to others and we rely on the impressions that others receive from us. Through a positive image, we can expect the acceptance and sympathy of others, improving the quality of life and more easily obtaining advantages, both materially and socially. Moreover, projecting a positive image generates favorable responses in others, contributing to strengthening our self-esteem and promoting mutual acceptance and integration. Therefore, it is possible to affirm that the image constitutes an essential element of human communication. Taking care of your image therefore becomes of primary importance for effective communication.

Self-image represents the individual perception of how one sees and evaluates oneself in a positive way. This judgment, whether positive or negative, is formed during childhood and continues to evolve throughout life, influenced by successes, failures, and from the feedback received from others.

Self-image does not always coincide with reality, tending to converge when we experience good self-esteem and self-efficacy.

This perception affects our behavior in several ways:

✓ Goals: A greater sense of self-efficacy translates into more ambitious goals.

✓ Motivation: Self-confidence determines persistence and commitment to tackling tasks, as well as providing resilience, the ability to learn from mistakes and tolerance for failure. Those who lack self-confidence tend to give in when faced with challenges.

✓ Emotions: Control of anxiety is strongly influenced by perceived self-efficacy. Those with a low sense of self-efficacy tend to interpret more situations as stressful, amplifying the severity of potential dangers.

✓ Decisions: Individuals with low self-efficacy limit the range of their possible performances and goals to pursue.

Self-image and perceived self-efficacy play a key role in determining our emotional well-being. This also impacts the perception of others towards us: those with good self-esteem manifest themselves with confidence, appearing more attractive and competent in the eyes of others.

How to improve our image in front of others?

To improve your perception of ourselves, it is important to avoid having a single, general image, but rather develop different ones based on situations and tasks. For example, feeling deficient in some activities does not automatically imply deficiencies in all others. It is essential to consider the specific circumstances of poor performance without drawing general conclusions.

Sometimes it is beneficial to set self-improvement goals that target your weaknesses to make a positive change in your self-image.

Being aware of our behaviors, verbal and non-verbal language, as well as the signals transmitted by our body, represents a truly crucial step in cultivating a positive self-image. We are often inclined to think that a winning image is linked to beauty physics. However, we all have experienced of being fascinated by people who do not necessarily possess attractive appearance. What attracts us to others is not just the physical appearance, but rather the personality and identity that the body expresses. This positive interiority becomes magnetic, translating into charm and charisma.

Charm is manifested through gestures, facial expressions, tone of voice and intensity of gaze.

The fundamental elements of charm undoubtedly include the gaze and the smile. Staring into the eyes of our interlocutor with a smile denotes a genuine interest in the person in front of us. The posture of the body and the way in which we position ourselves in space, in relation to others, are also important. Our external expression must reflect our authenticity and personality, which, if cultivated and enriched over time, influences our actions and behaviors, having a significant impact on relationships with others.

Another important element of effective communication: charisma

Charisma represents a magnetic aura that attracts attention and plays an essential role in persuasive communication. What does possessing charisma really mean and why is having this prerogative so relevant? And how can we strengthen our individual charisma?

Have you ever noticed those people who exude charm even before saying a word?

Just seeing them enter a room is enough to notice how they manage to capture the attention of everyone present, like a true cosmic focal point. When they speak, silence spreads among those around them, captured and entranced by their expressions. The question is: can we become people with these characteristics? Is charisma an innate gift or can it be cultivated and strengthened over time?

To begin, let's correctly define the concept of charisma. This quality represents the ability to charm, attract and persuade others. To be precise, charisma derives from the combination of three elements, the relationships among which influence the distinct styles present in charismatic people.

These three components include:

1. Energy: Represents an individual's ability to influence the surrounding environment.
2. Presence: Reflects the ability to give and receive attention. Charismatic people are able to pay attention to others and simultaneously attract attention when they are the center of attention.
3. Warmth: Indicates the ability to exert power and presence over others. Charisma is not limited to those with power and presence but extends to those who use their personal resources to support or promote causes that are important to us.

How to strengthen our charism?

Improving your charisma is essential not only for achieving personal and professional goals, but above all for communicating effectively and persuasively. Increasing our charisma allows us to:

✓ Be persuasive in business presentations, interviews or meetings.
✓ Attract attention in a positive way and leave a memorable impression.
✓ Earn respect and respect from our colleagues.
✓ Successfully manage a work group.
✓ Be a point of reference within our family or group of friends.

Now, that we understand the importance of having charisma, let's explore how you can develop it. To become charismatic people, it is crucial to recognize that charisma does not have a unique form. As author Olivia Fox Cabane points out in her renowned book "The Charisma Myth," there are four types of charisma:

1. The charisma of attention: Manifests itself when someone manages to make others feel good through their ability to listen with attention and respect.

2. Visionary charisma: comes from a total belief in an idea or cause, accompanied by the ability to inspire others to follow it.

3. The charisma of kindness: present in those who exude strong human warmth and possess high emotional intelligence.

4. The charisma of authority: represented by power and social status, often associated with dictators and generals of the past.

Understanding these four forms of charisma is the first step in cultivating and developing this characteristic so that it best reflects our values and inclinations.

How to develop the same qualities as charismatic people

Let's explore together the essential characteristics of a charismatic person and how it is possible to develop them to enhance one's charisma. The goal is to create an irresistible magnetism through clarity of objectives, resolve in challenges and inner peace, conveying the idea of being in the right place at the right time.

✓ Familiarize yourself with setting clear goals and aggressively pursuing them.

✓ You acquire a greater and fuller ability not to retreat in the face of challenges, becoming the person who finds solutions even when they seem invisible to others.

✓ Continuously nurture your talents by committing to training and constant improvement.

Create an aura of mystery

Every individual with charisma always maintains a veil of reserve that arouses curiosity and stimulates the imagination of others.

✓ In the work environment or with people of some importance to you, being open can be reassuring, but not necessarily charismatic.

✓ Instead of revealing details of your private life in the first ten minutes of conversation, listen carefully, understand the interests of your interlocutors and focus on intelligent contributions, thus making your conversation more fascinating and charismatic.

Live according to your values

In this case we could talk about holiness, but not of a religious type of holiness, but of that linked to one's lifestyles. Living according to one's values, one's ideals and one's beliefs without compromising, despite everything and everyone, gives the impression of enormous strength and freedom and, consequently, arouses enormous admiration.

✓ It's about identifying a series of values, habits and behaviors that we consider truly essential to improve the quality of our lives and our personal growth.

✓ Focus completely on these fundamental aspects for a few days, dedicating our attention and energy, and simplifying or eliminating everything else.

Eloquence

In addition to body language, charisma manifests itself mainly through the use of words. Our verbal expressions are deeply affecting. Therefore, developing the ability to use words and voice effectively, especially in public situations, represents an essential skill for increasing charisma.

When faced with a question that is asked of us, let's take a moment before answering rather than answering hastily. Overall, it's about developing the ability to speak thoughtfully, pausing when we obviously feel it's appropriate.

✓ Emotions should not be considered adversaries when speaking in public. On the contrary, let us always use them to our advantage, accentuating them if necessary and harnessing their energy in our speeches.

✓ We improve our breathing and vary the rhythm of our voice to make our speech more engaging.

✓ We enrich our conversations with evocative images, anecdotes, stories and rich language.

Stage presence

Charismatic people are distinguished by their notable presence. However, being theatrical, having a strong stage presence, does not necessarily imply adopting jester or Prima donna attitudes. Sometimes, a quiet composure can capture the attention of interlocutors more than forced exhibitionism.

The essential thing is to remain authentic since authenticity represents a key element of charisma.

Let's reflect first of all on what makes us more comfortable: speaking loudly or whispering, moving a lot or staying still, joking with listeners or maintaining a formal attitude? We always take note of the answers to discover our magic formula that will help make us more charismatic.